Create your own fish stories!

Nothing can bring a family together like a day of fishing. At **takemefishing.org**, discover a wealth of information on how to get started and where to go. Learn about selecting tackle, how to cast, boating safety and more.

Use **takemefishing.org** to find places to fish and boat in your hometown and across the nation. Search our state by state event listings to take part in free fishing days, boat shows and seminars close to you.

Visit **takemefishing.org** today!
You'll discover that fishing is easy, fun and affordable…
and a great way to make memories that will last a lifetime.

"takemefishing"

GET INFORMATION AND GET GOING AT
TAKEMEFISHING.ORG

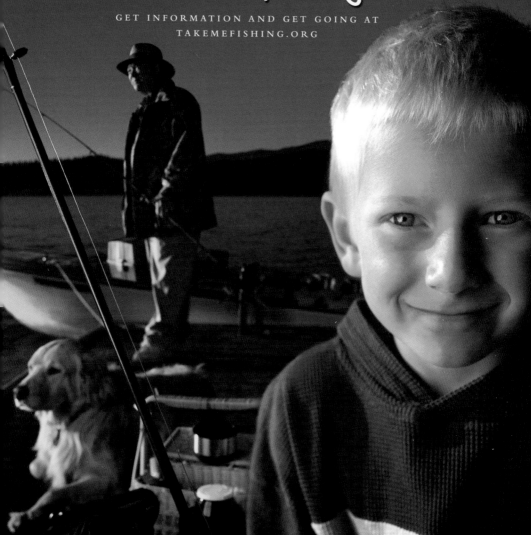

Celebrity Fish Talk

Tales of Fishing from an All-Star Cast

Dave Strege

Foreword by Kevin Costner

www.SportsPublishingLLC.com

ISBN: 1-58261-841-0

© 2005 by Dave Strege

Publishers: Peter L. Bannon and Joseph J. Bannon Sr.
Senior managing editor: Susan M. Moyer
Acquisitions editor: Noah A. Amstadter
Developmental editor: Regina D. Sabbia
Art director: K. Jeffrey Higgerson
Dust jacket design: Dustin J. Hubbart
Project managers: Jim Henehan and Greg Hickman
Imaging: Dustin J. Hubbart and Heidi Norsen
Photo editor: Erin Linden-Levy
Vice president of sales and marketing: Kevin King
Media and promotions managers: Courtney Hainline (regional),
        Randy Fouts (national), Maurey Williamson (print)

Printed in United States of America

Sports Publishing L.L.C.
804 North Neil Street
Champaign, IL 61820

Phone: 1-877-424-2665
Fax: 217-363-2073
Web site: www.SportsPublishingLLC.com

To my wife Cindy,
who prefers her fish on a plate rather than a hook.

And to my mom and dad, lifetime fishing partners
who can spin a few fishing tales of their own.

Contents

Foreword

Fishing is the smells of a canvas tent, an old Coleman stove and yellow salmon eggs. To this day, those smells are ingrained in my senses. I can't get rid of them nor do I want to. They bring me closer to nature, closer to God.

My biggest release is playing sports, but the most spiritual I get is when I'm on a stream. The solitude provides time to think, to reflect. Honestly, the whole ceremony surrounding a fishing trip brings me peace.

When I was a kid and my dad asked me what I wanted for my birthday, I'd say I wanted him to take me fishing. When a trip was planned, the ceremony began. The night before, I'd organize my tackle box like a girl would arrange her jewelry box. I was not a casual fisherman. I'd tie up hooks the night before, wanting to be prepared so as to maximize my fishing time. The sandwiches would be made the night before so we'd be ready to go in the morning. I'd go to bed but couldn't sleep. The anticipation and excitement were caffeine to my system. I wouldn't fall asleep until 2 or 3. My dad would wake me a couple of hours later and I'd be ready to go, right on time. I could be late for school or something else, but I was never late for fishing.

The memories are as fresh as the trout we ate around the campfire, where somehow the morning bacon always seemed to taste better. Sizzling bacon, the smell of salmon eggs, the anticipation—fishing is so many things.

It's the waffle houses you pass as you drive to the lake in the darkness. It's those small towns you ride through that either don't have a theater or a movie is showing that was in your city a year and a half ago. It's when the car leaves the highway and hits gravel. The sound tells you you're closer to fishing. It's driving around the bend and hoping you don't see someone sitting in your favorite spot. It's finding a stick with a good "Y" on it. It's a stringer of bluegill, which can be just as precious as a 150-pound sailfish. It's the mystery of a red lure catching all the fish. It's sitting next to a guy who has a red lure and you don't. That's fishing.

It's not always as pure as a fly fisherman gently casting a dry fly to a German brown. Sometimes it's a red bobber, a hunk of cheese and a big, ugly catfish. Seeing that bobber go under can be as exciting as watching a trout kissing the surface where your fly sits.

Fishing is talking to someone else who knows fishing. That's like being in a foreign country and running into somebody who speaks your language. Fishing is adventurous and challenging. It's the unexpected. It's about falling in and getting wet.

It's about enjoying a perfect day, whether you catch fish or not.

Catching fish isn't a prerequisite for a successful fishing trip. Some people think it is. They just don't get it. Many trips I've taken didn't produce a single fish. I feel a measure of disappointment, yet the experience only increases my desire to return. Really, I think there's a fishing god and he says, "To be a real fisherman, you've got to appreciate the days you don't catch fish. So I'm going to make you earn it." Sometimes fishermen don't catch fish. They just don't.

Anglers often lament about the one that got away, but the one they do land can be cherished for a lifetime. The unforgettable memory of the fish is what makes fishing great. A real fisherman can relate. A real fisherman doesn't exaggerate. Fishing is a little bit like golf. In golf, there's a gentleman's agreement about not touching or moving your ball. That's a true golfer. Conversely, a true fisherman does not tell tall fish tales. Some people catch or even lose a fish that grows bigger with each retelling of the story. I don't do that. I don't turn a one-pound fish into a 20-pound fish. A true fisherman doesn't lie about it because he can't. A true fisherman tells and treasures a genuine fishing story.

—Kevin Costner

Preface

As an outdoors writer, I have reported many fishing tales, some comical and others beyond belief, like a hooked marlin jumping into a boat and a fisherman surviving after getting pulled overboard by a huge tuna while strapped into a rod harness.

Books have been written about wild fishing stories, but it occurred to me that none came with a celebrity angle. The rich and famous fish, too, so why wouldn't they have a tale to spin? So the idea for *Celebrity Fish Talk* was spawned.

Kevin Costner is a fraternity brother of mine from Cal State Fullerton in Southern California. We fished together in college, once catching our largemouth bass limits at Lake Cachuma near Santa Barbara.

I was into bass fishing and the use of a depth finder to find underwater structure. When I located a long, underwater point, I threw a plastic buoy overboard to mark the spot. Costner had never seen this before. He thought I had gone mad.

But once we turned around and started trolling along this "invisible" point, we started catching fish. Costner describes himself as an innate fisherman. That day he learned the scientific methodology to fishing.

Fishing is in Costner's blood no matter what the technique. He even enjoys spearfishing, incidentally. I figured who better to ask if the celebrity angle would fly than he? When I asked his opinion, he didn't hesitate. He embraced the idea, gave me his blessing and support, and cast me out among his peers.

Great, now what?

Kevin Costner and Dave Strege hold a pair of largemouth bass limits taken from Cachuma Lake in June 1976, before catch and release became popular.

Photo courtesy of Dave Strege

Well, I needed stories. Unfortunately, gaining access to celebrities wasn't as easy as standing on the red carpet at the Academy Awards with a microphone in my hand.

I searched high and low for all the celebrity events I could find and gain access to, and started my collection. Mostly I attended celebrity pro-am golf tournaments, such as the Bob Hope in La Quinta and the AT&T in Pebble Beach. I figured if they swing a golf club, maybe they cast a fishing plug, too.

The driving range was a perfect stage for a quick interview. The atmosphere was relaxed, it was away from the crowds and there usually was time to kill before teeing off. I approached every celebrity I could. Some I knew were fishermen, others I had no idea. To those, I'd simply approach cold and ask.

Imagine walking up to Jack Nicholson sitting alone in a golf cart waiting for a tournament to start. Or following Clint Eastwood into the celebrity-only hospitality tent at the AT&T before getting kicked out. Eastwood half agreed to talk to me the day before but all I ultimately got was a Dirty Harry, what-do-*you*-want? look. Needless to say, Eastwood didn't make my day. Nor did Nicholson. Neither offered up stories.

"I'm not the guy for that," Nicholson said.

OK, then, thanks anyway. Sorry to bother you.

Really, it *was* OK. I understand the privacy thing with celebrities. Their private time is golden and I respected that. For many, their fishing stories are the only thing the public doesn't know about them. Who can blame them for wanting to keep *something* sacred?

In many cases, some were simply not fishermen. President Gerald Ford said he wasn't into fishing, that he was always more into team sports. Flanked by two Secret Service men, Ford then walked off the driving range in preparation to play golf, an individual sport. *Fore!*

Hey, Michael Jordan, just wondering, have you ever been fishing?

"No, never have."

How about you Sean Connery, do you fish?

"No, I'm sorry."

Thanks, anyway.

Some celebrities said they don't fish but like to eat fish. *Bon appetit.*

Thankfully, for all the celebrities who didn't have a fishing story, didn't fish or didn't care to divulge a story, several other famous people were out there who agreed to let their guard down and share an experience.

Hopefully, the tales will offer a glimpse of their lives that have never been seen before. Hopefully, the stories will amuse and amaze but most of all entertain.

As a means of introducing and complementing the stories, I incorporated narratives that relate what the topic is for each chapter.

Among them, I describe what took place behind the scenes in Robert Redford's popular fly-fishing movie *A River Runs Through It*. I talk about fish smells, funny game warden stories and practical jokes among anglers. I write about those who are passionate about fishing. I describe the dangers of fishing and how that angler survived being pulled overboard by a huge tuna. I tell how a spearfisherman survived a shark attack. I talk about fishing presidents, memorable moments and the ones that got away.

The journey I've taken has been long, fun, tiring, disappointing, uplifting, discouraging, encouraging, gratifying, tedious—did I mention long?—monotonous and educational.

I found many famous people to be down-to-earth, genuinely nice, such as Jay Leno, Samuel L. Jackson, Andy Garcia, Vince Gill, General Norman Schwarzkopf, Bobby Knight, Matt Lauer, Pat O'Brien, Nancy O'Dell and Curt Gowdy.

Something else I discovered: Many celebrities are just like average Joe Angler. They enjoy fishing, and they have a fish story.

As former tennis great Michael Chang told me when I first began this project years ago, "Anyone who loves fishing always has some kind of fish stories."

Hope you enjoy them.

Acknowledgments

To the celebrities who sacrificed a few minutes to share their favorite fish story, I give a huge and sincere thank you. I couldn't have done it without you.

Kevin Costner forfeited more than just a few minutes. He gave up several hours, supporting my project in more ways than one. He liked the idea from the start and his encouragement helped push me forward. Many thanks, Kevin.

To the game wardens, anglers, divers, shark experts, outdoor TV personalities and everybody else who helped me create colorful introductory narratives for each chapter, I am grateful.

To my literary agent, Faye Bender. You put the polish on the project with your guidance and suggestions. Without those, this never would have happened. I'm so glad we hooked up. You're the best.

Thanks also to Sports Publishing for an awesome job. You folks are a class act and a joy to work with.

My wife Cindy put up with my taking vacation time to traipse to various celebrity golf tournaments in Palm Springs, Monterey, Los Angeles and Lake Tahoe to collect stories. She's a great supporter. Thank you, honey.

My brother John Strege, author and expert wordsmith for *Golf World* and *Golf Digest* magazines, always encouraged and believed in me from beginning to end. Thanks for everything, John.

To the numerous public relations people who work behind the scenes to facilitate media coverage at golf tournaments and who allowed me access for my project, I can't thank you enough. In particular, a special thanks to Toby Zwikel and Steve Brener of Brener Zwikel & Associates, the best media relations guys around.

And to all my family and friends, much obliged for all the support. I'm hoping it was worth waiting for.

Author's Note

Tiger Woods, Deion Sanders and the U.S. presidents were the only celebrities whose stories I obtained through press conferences, media reports, books or police reports. All other celebrities I interviewed personally.

The quote from Woods talking about fishing in "Fishing Lines and Bloopers" is courtesy of *Golf Digest*.

Chapter One

Poetry with a Fly Rod

P ull on a pair of waders, pick up a fly rod and step into a trout stream. This is the world of fly fishing, where nature sings a melody that is salve for the soul.

Water trickles over and around rocks in a soothing sonnet that melts stress. Birds chirp in the trees nearby. A trout nips at a fly atop the surface on an otherwise quiet pool. A cloud of mayflies buzzes overhead.

Civilization and the troubles of the world are a million miles away. You meld with nature and begin to paint on a living canvas. The rod is the brush and the strokes are smooth, graceful, artistic. The line floats through the air, unrolls on the water and delivers the artificial fly to its intended target.

The current whisks the line downstream toward the feeding trout. A slurp on the surface indicates a strike. The rod is pulled upward with

Director Robert Redford looks through the eyepiece for a scene that depicts Norman Maclean fly fishing, as played by Craig Sheffer.
Photo by John Kelly

one hand, the line pulled downward with the other, like an orchestra leader directing a climactic finish.

The fish is hooked. The rainbow trout frantically races left and then right. It tires and is subdued. Quickly and gently, the hook is removed. The squirming fish is released and it darts for calm water to recuperate.

Another trout rises to gulp a real fly, advertising its presence in the pool. Another cast, another fish, another inoculation of repose. It's a good day. No, it's a *great* day. Exhilarating. Stimulating. Rewarding.

Fly fishing is often called the purest form of fishing, probably because art and nature merge in a symmetry offered by no other style of fishing. It is revered among those with a fly rod.

Nowhere is the deepest meaning of fly fishing more evident or more alluring than in the 1992 movie *A River Runs Through It*, based on the book by Norman Maclean.

In the film we learn that Reverend Maclean (Tom Skerritt) taught his sons Norman (Craig Sheffer) and Paul (Brad Pitt) as much about fly fishing as he did about all other spiritual matters. "In our family, there was no clear line between religion and fly fishing," Norman says in an early scene.

Fly fishing is depicted as a common bond among the Maclean men. Coupled with the poetic "shadow casting," beautiful Montana scenery and a call of the wild, *A River Runs Through It* became a natural advertisement for fly fishing.

Thirteen million anglers are fly fishers and many were inspired to become one after seeing the movie. The classic film, directed by Robert Redford, was a boon to the fly-fishing industry largely because of its realism. The producers did their best to depict the sport as it was in the 1920s and to remain politically correct in the use of real trout as actors.

In the spirit of modern fly fishing, the movie makers tried to ensure that the fish used in the film were eventually released alive. After the credits, this message appears: "No fish were killed or injured during the making of *A River Runs Through It*. The producers would like to point out that, although the Macleans kept their catch as was common earlier in this century, enlightened fishermen today endorse a 'catch and release' policy to assure that this priceless resource swims free to fight another day. Good fishing."

As it turned out, a few trout did give their lives—one could say it was for a good cause—and not all the rainbow trout in the movie were real. In one underwater scene, about two seconds long, a mechanical trout on an underwater track is used to depict the trophy rainbow rising to the fly Paul presents.

This *is* Hollywood, after all.

As pure as the movie portrays fly fishing, *A River Runs Through It* has an interesting edge below the surface. With any Hollywood film, numerous people work feverishly behind the scenes to ensure a seamless production, and this one was no different.

John Dietsch, a former fly-fishing guide who had gotten into film making, was hired as the fly-fishing production coordinator. He was responsible for making the actors and scenes look authentic.

Before filming, Dietsch took Pitt and Sheffer to a Santa Monica, California park several times to teach them fly casting. Getting them to experience what a fish felt like at the end of the line was a bit trickier.

John Dietsch demonstrates fly-casting technique to Craig Sheffer while John Bailey and Jerry Siem (fly-fishing advisers) look on from behind.
Photo by John Kelly

One time, Dietsch took the end of Pitt's fishing line, gave it to a little boy and told him to take off running.

"What are you doing?" Pitt asked.

"That's what it's like to play a fish," Dietsch explained.

By the time shooting began on the river, the actors were adept at fly casting. Nevertheless, a double was hired for the casting scenes. Jason Borger, the son of renowned fly fisher Gary Borger, is the same size as Pitt, Sheffer and Skerritt, and made for an ideal stunt man. It was Borger who was filmed "shadow casting" from atop a rock, looking like a maestro.

Borger resembled an amateur fly fisher, however, in the first take of the first scene he was in. The first cast he made went into a willow tree.

Cut!

"I think we'll be sending that one back to your father," Redford joked.

Another blooper occurred away from the camera and crew during a break in shooting. On occasion, Dietsch would take the actors fly fishing to keep them sharp. One time, Pitt impaled himself in the back of the neck with the fly he was attempting to cast. The hook dug under the skin and the barb did its job by not letting go.

"Just pull it out, Dietsch, just pull it out!" Pitt exclaimed. "Pull it out!"

So Dietsch did. He pulled out the hook, along with two and a half inches of skin.

"It's one of those horror stories as a guide," Dietsch says. "It's never happened before. ...It was not pretty."

While the actors knew how to fly cast, catching a fish on the fly was as foreign as French. No matter how good the fly caster, hookups are not guaranteed.

In a Hollywood production, the movie maker might wait as an actor puts on weight to play a certain character, but Redford didn't have a lifetime so the actors could become proficient fly fishermen. Nor could he afford the actors the many hours on the water it might take just for them to experience a hookup and fighting a fish on the fly.

So to hurriedly acquaint them to a fighting trout, Dietsch took them to a private pond on rancher Ted Watson's property in Livingston, Montana.

Watson's pond was the perfect solution. Hookups were virtually guaranteed. The trout are fed with grain pellets. So Dietsch took a Hare's

*The shadow cast. Stand-in Jason Borger performs
the shadow cast for Brad Pitt's character.*
Photo by John Kelly

Ear fly and cut off the hackle. The fly then looked like a grain pellet. In fly-fishing parlance, he matched the hatch. A handful of grain pellets were tossed into the pond and the water erupted into a piranha-like feeding frenzy. When it died down, Dietsch instructed Pitt to make a cast.

"As soon as that Hare's Ear drops, a big fish comes up and just bangs it, and then he got to feel what it's like to fight a fish," Dietsch says. "Brad and Craig Sheffer caught two or three fish that day in a matter of 15 minutes."

It was Watson's pond from which trout were recruited as actors for the fishing scenes. Dietsch and others would catch the trout and put them in a creek cordoned off by a seine net. The trout would easily be scooped up and transported in a stocking truck to the river on shooting days. They would be returned to the pond after filming.

The film's signature scene was when Pitt's character hooks a trophy rainbow trout and is dragged down river, fighting the fish and the rapids. Several trout in the 10-pound class were needed for the climax when Paul holds up the fish to show his father and brother. Not wanting to harm or kill one fish, they planned to alternate between 10 trout about the same size. So that's how many were caught and placed in the holding creek at Watson's. The next morning when Dietsch arrived to transport the large trout to the shooting location, he made an alarming discovery. Somebody had removed the netting. The big fish were back swimming in the pond.

"On one level, I was scared to death," Dietsch says. "I just couldn't show up on the set with no fish, I would've been fired. At the same time, being a fisherman, there's a challenge. It's perhaps the most epic challenge of my fishing career."

Time was of the essence. Big trout were needed. Fast.

"So there was this big panic," Jason Borger recalls. "Of course, when you want to catch fish, you never can. We wound up having to use one female and one male fish for the scene because that's all we could get."

The difference between the two fish is as clear as the Gallatin River, where much of the film was shot. In the front view of Pitt holding the fish, the rainbow is a male with a dark, hooked jaw. From the rear view, the rainbow is a female with a rounded, white jaw.

"If you look for it, you can see it," Dietsch says.

The difference is subtle and not recognizable by an unsuspecting eye. Certainly it isn't as obvious as a boom microphone popping into a scene from above.

In one of the many special effects of Hollywood, a plastic milk carton served as a stand-in for the trophy trout that Paul battles in the rapid. The carton was filled with water and rocks, tied to the end of the line and tossed into the river. This made the fly rod bend and act as if a real fish were at the other end.

And that wasn't Pitt in the rapid trying to reel in the trophy milk carton. It was Dietsch.

When Dietsch suggested the idea of the rapid scene to Redford, the director asked him to demonstrate it. The next day, Dietsch put on a wetsuit and jumped into the river with a fly rod in hand as a rescue team observed closely from the bank.

"Redford loved it, so they brought in a Hollywood stuntman," Dietsch says. "The guy didn't look like he knew what we was doing. He wasn't a fisherman."

So Dietsch was asked to do it. "That's how I got into the Screen Actor's Guild," he says.

Pitt was in the river, too, for close-up shots. But he was close to shore out of harm's way. Dietsch was in the dangerous whitewater. They asked him to do five takes. So essentially, he risked his life five times. On the second take, the milk carton got stuck in an eddy and when the line tightened, Dietsch was turned around and pushed under the surface of the water for a few seconds.

"Of course, I felt like I'd blown it," Dietsch says. "We did it three more times and they got what they needed."

But the impromptu disappearing act became a big part of the sequence. The editor loved it so much that more scenes were shot to get the father and son looking at the river with nobody in it.

The poignant moment at the end of the scene was no accident, however. Paul has a smile as wide as the river, and Norman and Reverend Maclean admire him and his fish with reverence. "You are a fine fisherman," the reverend tells his son.

"I think the reason the movie captured the world's imagination is that rivers speak to us," Dietsch says. "That's what Norman said. The river has words and beneath the rocks are words and those words speak to us. I think Norman and Robert were able to impart that to audiences so people who never fished before and people who do fish got it. It became the Holy Grail because everybody can sort of connect to what it's like to be out there with your brother or dad.

"And there's a certain solace we get by standing in the river and simply being."

For the artisan of the river, catching fish becomes secondary. In the least, the salve doesn't require the likes of Paul's trophy trout. Catching wild trout no bigger than your hand is just as exciting. I've been fortunate to have caught chum salmon to 12 pounds on streamer flies on the Alagnak River in Alaska. I've felt the thrill of a big fish caught on the fly, experienced the exuberance of Paul in *A River Runs Through It*.

But wild rainbows measuring three to eight inches can provide the same amount of voltage as its bigger salmonoid brethren. Amazingly, I found these electrifying small fry only an hour away from the 10 million people that live in the Greater Los Angeles Area.

High in the mountains above the city of Azusa, the west fork of the San Gabriel River has a catch-and-release-only section with wild rainbow trout. I pedaled my bicycle a few miles up an adjoining road and found myself lost in seclusion.

Trees stood as sentinels, guarding my spot from intrusion and providing shade. Birds chirped. A squirrel rustled some leaves. Insects flew overhead. A trout pecked at the surface, another insect devoured. The stereophonic sounds of water were hypnotic. Mother Nature held me in her arms, and all was right with the world.

"Eventually," Norman Maclean says, "all things merge into one and a river runs through it."

MATT LAUER

One day while fly fishing the Bighorn River in Montana, Matt Lauer was swept away down river, just as Paul Maclean in *A River Runs Through It*.

The life-long trout fisherman was enjoying the most incredible fishing day of his life, catching German brown trout and rainbow trout one after another, until a big brown seemingly caught *him*.

"I stepped off a little sand bar and went into fairly fast-moving water in my waders and started to float down," the *Today* show host recalls. "Of course, my guide is floating alongside of me in the boat. I went probably 100 yards, trying to hold my rod above my head.

"We finally got into some flat water. I tried to get into the boat and I said, 'Here, hold my rod.' The guide said, 'I can't hold your rod. If I hold your rod, you don't land the fish.'"

Whether the guide felt it was unlucky or was just taking the "pure" in fly fishing to the extreme, Lauer did not know. If it were a world record, then it might make sense. International Game Fish Association rules state an angler must not receive help in landing a fish or it is disqualified from record consideration.

But this was no record.

"Literally, he made me climb into the boat holding the rod in one hand," Lauer says. "I looked like the Michelin Tire Man because my waders were filled with water. I rolled over into the boat and landed the fish."

As he did with the other fish, Lauer released the 22-inch brown trout back into the river. Then he did the most logical thing he could do. He emptied his waders.

TIGER WOODS

Kodiak Island in Alaska has one of the highest densities of bears in the world, so it wasn't surprising that Tiger Woods and his threesome would encounter one of them.

Woods took time off after the 2001 U.S. Open to go fly fishing for king salmon with his Orlando, Florida neighbors and fellow golf professionals Mark O'Meara and John Cook.

During a press conference before the 2001 PGA Championship, Woods described what happened when a nine-foot brown bear started after them.

"I had already caught a king salmon and was down by the raft when Mark landed a king. With John's help, he dragged the fish along a grassy trail toward the raft when Cookie yelled out, 'There's a bear!'

"So they tried to hurry back across the river and there was a good current, so it was going to take time, and the bear was in hot pursuit because he could smell the fish that Mark had dragged along the ground.

"It was coming right at us. They got to the raft, threw the fish in and then jumped in themselves. If they hadn't got back in time, I would have thrown my fish at the bear.

"We were all right. We're still here.

"The fishing was incredible and we had a great time."

LEE HORSLEY

Lee Horsley never intended to make a fashion statement with fishing jewelry. Earrings never were his thing, until one day while fly fishing.

Horsley was daydreaming about his career, and how viewers were getting younger, and how those younger viewers were piercing their ears and noses.

With his mind wandering, Horsley kept casting from a boat off Malibu, California, trying to catch a calico bass with a mackerel-pattern fly on a saltwater fly rod.

"I'm thinking about my work and what I do for a living as an actor," explains Horsley, best known for his television roles as Matt Houston and Nero Wolfe in the early 1980s.

"I'm trying to cast this thing out as far as I can, and the wind is messing it up. I'm thinking, 'OK, the viewing audience is getting a lot younger, Lee.' I'm thinking all these guys have rings in their noses and rings in their ears and everything else, and I don't get it.

"The next thing I know, I've thrown that mackerel pattern into the back of my ear, and I pierced my ear."

It was a perfect piercing. The hook went clean through the earlobe, right where you'd put an earring.

Needless to say, Horsley didn't care for the new look and removed the mackerel-pattern earring immediately.

"The hole closed up nicely," he says.

EVEL KNIEVEL

Evel Knievel walked out onto Berkeley Pier in San Francisco Bay wearing waders and carrying a fly rod, as if he were ready to fish a river in Montana.

No, it wasn't done on a dare. Knievel was just a kid and knew nothing about ocean fishing or fishing from a pier. That was obvious, since his fly line barely reached the water.

"So I'm out there fishing and I catch this fish that weighed about a pound," the former daredevil recalls. "I said to this guy down the walkway, 'Boy, I've got a beauty, what the heck is it?' He told me, 'That's what we use for bait.'

"I looked in his basket and he's got two, 25- or 30-pound fish in there. He said, 'Where the heck you get them fishing boots?' I said, 'Well, I'm from Montana.' He said, 'You don't need them boots around here, you don't go into the water.'

"The water was about 30 feet deep and here I had a pair of waders on. Anyway, I got a quick fishing lesson that day."

MAURY POVICH

Maury Povich, a novice angler in June 1998, visited Montana with his wife, seeking to experience the quintessence of fishing.

"We went up near Glacier National Park, which is marvelous, and fished on the Flathead River," the TV host relates. "I wanted to learn fly fishing because I'm told fly fishing is to fishing like sailing is to boating. It's supposed to be the purest form.

"It was marvelous, but the problem was, my wife caught more fish than I did. The guy told me afterward that women are better fly fishermen than men. I said, 'Why?' And he said, 'Because they have patience and they're not macho about it.'

"She caught a rainbow and a cutthroat and I only caught a cutthroat. In fact, I caught my cutthroat in the belly.

"My wife said, 'I told you who the man in the house was.'"

Povich's wife, of course, is nationally acclaimed newscaster Connie Chung.

"She was very proud of her catch," Povich adds.

JOHN O'HURLEY

The trout weren't biting and the fly-fishing episode was about to become a bust until a producer tipped an artificial fly with a little worm.

For pure fly fishermen, this is sacrilegious, using bait on a fly. Worse, when a fish was finally caught, it was kept so they could catch it again and again in order to fill an episode.

"We never released the fish," says actor John O'Hurley, a guest on the fishing show. "We had to catch him three times because they needed to get some footage. The poor fish, he was pretty tired. It was the same fish and, of course, you had to say, 'Ooh, good fish, good fish,' every time."

O'Hurley, known as J. Peterman to fans of the TV hit *Seinfeld*, is an accomplished fly fisher, yet he played along. But he refused to reveal the show's name, the network or even the name of the top-notch guide.

"I don't even want to name where it was," he says. "I want to keep it as anonymous as possible. I felt so bad."

JENNIFER SAVIDGE

Jennifer Savidge was new to fly fishing when she took a friend to Alpers' fly-fishing ranch on the Owens River near Mammoth Lakes, California.

Savidge, known for her TV roles on *St. Elsewhere* and *JAG*, was going to teach Katie Mitchell an art she had yet to master herself.

Fishing from a wooden bridge, Savidge saw a trout up stream and cast to it several times with a dry fly. The trout wouldn't rise to the fly.

Mitchell was using a nymph, which sinks, so Savidge instructed her to cast it above the trout and let it float down, and she did—perfectly. The trout engulfed the fly.

Then the inexplicable occurred. Savidge turned savage.

"I was so excited, I knocked her down off the bridge and grabbed her rod," Savidge says. "Suddenly, I looked at her and she had this shocked expression on her face. I thought, 'Oh my God, I'm acting just like those macho guys that shove the women out of the way.'"

Embarrassed, Savidge gave the rod back to Mitchell and allowed her the joy of bringing in the trout and of laughing at Savidge as she netted the fish.

When Savidge leaned over with the net, everything fell out of the pockets of her fishing vest.

"I hadn't zipped up the pockets in my vest because I was such a pig about getting this trout out of her hands," she says. "It was greed personified. I wanted it."

The actress has since become an accomplished fly fisher, a much more *civilized* fly fisher.

HUEY LEWIS

Huey Lewis stalked the river on his Montana ranch for years in hopes of catching a trophy German brown trout. So what happened the one day he finally spotted his dream fish?

The rock star was ill prepared to catch it. He was like a musician showing up for a concert without his instrument.

On this day in 1996, Lewis was playing fishing guide to three friends, who were outfitted with all of Huey's equipment.

So Lewis, wearing slacks and a brand-new pair of hiking boots, stood on the shore and pointed out to his friends where to cast.

When he spotted a big brown, he instructed Susan (not her real name) on how to cast to it, but Susan was not adept at fly fishing. Lewis told her to mend the line. To Susan, that probably meant repairing the line instead of flipping it up current.

Finally, she told Lewis to try it himself. So he did.

"From shore, I made the perfect cast and hooked the fish," Lewis says. "I'd never caught a 24-inch brown before and I was thinking this could be the fish."

But without waders or even a net, Lewis, anchored to shore, was unable to avoid the ensuing chaos and make a clean catch.

Upon Huey's instruction, Alan (not his real name) came over with his net and the horror began.

"This fish went up stream 100 yards—whoa!" Lewis recalls. "Now he was coming right at me and I was taking up the slack as fast as I could. I saw it was a big fish and you know what? I thought it might be 24 inches. Alan was out in the stream and he was fishing around with the net and slamming it over the fish's head."

Another friend with a net joined Alan and took a swipe at the fish. Huey's nerves frayed like fishing line pulled over sharp rocks.

"They weren't fluent in netting," Lewis deadpans. "I was sure we were going to break the fish off. So I grabbed the net and I launched into the stream with my new hiking boots—which are ruined to this day—and I netted it myself."

Finally, his dream came true, despite the nightmarish mayhem. Lewis measured the fish—it was 24 inches—and released it.

"That's my biggest brown trout on a dry fly," he says proudly. "It was really exciting."

Fortunately, Lewis could afford a new pair of boots.

MARTIN MILNER

They waved and hollered frantically for Martin Milner to come down river to avoid a confrontation that would have been unbearable.

Upwind and upriver on the Kenai River in Alaska, Milner couldn't quite make out the warnings from host John Barrett and the crew of ESPN's *Fly Fishing the World*.

Actor Martin Milner with a nice German brown.
Photo courtesy of Martin Milner

"I thought, 'OK, I'll work my way down there, the fishing must be better down there, so that's why they want me down there,'" says Milner, who starred on *Adam 12* as officer Pete Malloy. "So I kept fishing and was slowly working my way down."

Again the group beckoned Milner to come to them. Again Milner returned a quizzical look. Then they started pointing upstream from Milner.

"I looked and there was this bear in the river," Milner says. "He was swimming in the river upstream from me. All I could see was the big head of this Alaskan grizzly bear. He was not interested in me, but the current was carrying him right down to me."

The river delivered the bear to within 20 yards of Milner, who believed this was a little too close for comfort. Immediately panicking, he made a mad dash to safety.

But like a track star stumbling out the blocks, Milner slipped on some rocks and fell into the water. He scrambled to his feet and finally made it to shore without the bear giving chase.

The bear lumbered off into the woods, and a relieved Milner was given dry clothes so he could continue fishing.

The entire episode was captured on film, but despite Milner giving Barrett approval to use the footage, Barrett didn't have the heart.

"I don't want to use it, because there was such a look of terror on your face, I don't want to embarrass you," Barrett told Milner.

"So you don't see me falling in the show," Milner says. "You just see in the next sequence that I've got different clothes on."

Chapter Two

Stop, You're Under Arrest

Fishermen are notorious for a vivid exaggeration. A fish the size of a guppy suddenly becomes a trophy catch worth hanging on the wall. Among anglers, this stretching of the truth about a fish is as common as whiskers on a catfish. What's the crime?

No fishing regulation we know of deals with such lies. Fish and game codes aren't written to protect a fisherman's credibility. They are established to protect wildlife, to help prevent a fish species from following the dinosaur into extinction.

Rivers, lakes and oceans would get fished out without fishing regulations. Without rules, dishonest anglers would be clear to run amok, looting the fishery like criminals.

Unfortunately, despite regulations and game wardens sent into the field to enforce them, some anglers continue to step over the line. They commit various infractions such as fishing without a license, catching more than a limit, fishing out of season, fishing on private property, keeping undersized fish or snagging fish.

Many do it even when they know it is illegal. Oh, sure, some infractions are committed out of honest ignorance, yet countless other cases only serve as evidence that a good number of fishermen are not exactly honest.

Of course, telling a fib to friends about a certain catch is one thing. But lying to a game warden to cover tracks leading to an infraction is another story and often, it's a funny one.

The fishing world is filled with Pinocchios, and the excuses and cover-ups can be downright hysterical, along the lines of a child reporting his homework eaten by the family dog.

Sergeant Ed Johnson of the Maryland Natural Resources Police told of the time several years ago when he was on patrol in a marked police vessel in the Middle River in Baltimore County. It was spring and the bass were biting. He noticed a young gentleman fishing from shore. He watched him in the act of fishing for several minutes before finally approaching him.

The young man saw the warden coming, reeled in quickly and abruptly took off. Johnson caught up with him and asked to see his fishing license.

"His reply was not quite what I expected," Johnson says.

With a straight face and a demeanor as serious as someone taking a lie-detector test, the young man replied, "Sir, I was not fishing, I was teaching this worm how to swim."

The young man received high marks from Johnson for originality but was issued a citation for fishing without a license nevertheless.

Another angler accidentally turned his worm into an earring while trying to weasel his way out of a citation on the Green River in Utah.

Ted Gardiner, an enforcement officer for the Utah Division of Wildlife Resources, noticed the fisherman pulling worms out of his pocket, baiting a hook and casting it out. He also observed the man catch a trout and toss it into the weeds.

This wouldn't have been so bad had it not been on a particular stretch of the river where it was artificial flies and lures only, and fish between 15 to 20 inches were required to be released.

When the man saw Gardiner approach, he went into a fly-fishing routine with his spinning outfit, waving his baited hook back and forth through the air, pretending to be a fly fisherman.

"How's fishing?" Gardiner asked.

"Pretty good," the angler replied. "I'm using these flies."

"With a spinning rod?" Gardiner asked.

At that moment, the "fly fisher" accidentally hooked himself in the earlobe. For a couple of seconds, the worm dangled from his ear. The bait and hook were unmistakable.

Oops.

Believing the warden didn't see him, he quickly rubbed the worm off the hook and removed the hook from his ear. The angler was acting like a trophy trout trying to shake the hook free. He was fighting hard trying to get away. He was not giving up. No sir, he had an explanation for why that hook was bare, why his fly no longer looked like a fly.

"I've caught so many fish," he explained, "it wore all the feathers off the hook."

Uh, nice try.

Gardiner then reeled in his victim by having him empty the contents of his pocket. Once he did this, it was difficult for the angler not to admit his guilt. After all, the evidence was wiggling. He was cited for using bait on artificial-only water and for unlawful possession of an illegal-sized trout.

That 16-inch trout was supposed to be returned to the river unharmed, having fallen within the "slot limit."

Double oops.

In Idaho, a man was receiving a ticket for using a lure with barbed hooks on the Lower Salmon River, the *Idaho Wildlife On-Line Magazine* reported. The angler kept telling the game wardens that he never fished with barbed hooks and said something like, "Somebody must have stolen my rod, used it and returned it, but left the barbed hooks on it!"

Honestly, what do these anglers think, that game wardens were born yesterday? It's unbelievable the things people say and do.

One report in the Texas Parks and Wildlife Game Warden Field Notes told of a fisherman who cut off two inches of tail so an oversized black drum would be the legal size of 30 inches.

Another told of a time a game warden warned an angler who was getting ready to fish a trout lake that he needed a fishing license and trout stamp. He had neither. A little while later, the man was fishing anyway. He told the warden he thought he had received a verbal warning and could finish his trip.

Then there were the three guys on the shoreline at Lake Fork in Texas. Two of them claimed they weren't fishing, apparently because they didn't have fishing licenses. But when wardens noted a large amount of fishing gear, they looked in the van and saw fresh Polaroid snapshots of all three men—in the act of fishing.

The Kodak moment lives.

In many cases, a fisherman's guilt is simply uncovered by a child's innocence.

Several years ago, Gardiner was checking four adults and two children coming out of the back-country of Boulder Mountain. The brook trout they caught were iced down with snow in a cooler. They had caught 32 fish—full limits.

"Daddy," a five-year-old piped up at the wrong time. "Aren't you going to show him the fish in the sleeping bag?"

Busted.

Wrapped in a burlap sack and stuffed into a sleeping bag were an additional 32 brook trout. Citations all around.

The Texas Parks and Wildlife Game Warden Field Notes reported a warden walking up to an angler to ask if the fish were biting. Just as the man was responding that they weren't having any luck, his six-year-old son said excitedly, "Do you want to see our fish?"

Sure, Mr. Game Warden would love to see your fish.

So the boy led Mr. Warden to where dad had stowed a five-gallon bucket filled with 23 undersized speckled trout.

Don't kids say the darnedest things?

Andy Savland, a game warden in Alaska, related the time he was patrolling a local creek in Southeast Alaska and came upon a father and his five-year-old daughter. Dad was carrying a 30-pound king salmon while the daughter struggled to carry the fishing rod. When Savland met them, the dad put the fish down to give his arm a rest.

"Where'd you catch the fish?" asked Savland, wondering what part of the river produced the big king.

"Right here," the little girl answered before dad could say a word.

The girl was pointing to a snag mark near the tail. Snagging is illegal in freshwater, so Savland asked again.

"Where?"

Proudly, the girl pointed at the tail a second time and said, "Right here."

"I looked up at the father, whose jaw was nearly on the ground next to the fish," Savland says. "He simply said, 'Looks like we've got a problem.'"

The man received a citation and a lecture on sportsmanship and ethics.

Average Joe Angler isn't the only one that finds himself on the wrong end of the law. One time, a prominent outdoors TV personality breached an unwritten code of ethics and violated a fishing regulation, though he maintains his innocence.

In 1999 while filming an episode for ESPN's *The Hunt for the Big Fish*, host Larry Dahlberg caught an 18-pound steelhead on the Kitimat River in British Columbia and released the fish. Nothing wrong with that.

But when he released the fish, the hook was still in the fish's mouth and Dahlberg proceeded to catch the fish again. Once he landed the fish, he released it again. With the hook still in it. Finally, he landed the fish a third time and a game warden yelled for him to release the fish. *Without the hook.*

Two wardens charged him under Section 4 of the B.C. sportfishing regulations that states "No person shall injure or molest a fish."

Dahlberg contends he was doing no such thing. He and his crew were attempting to get more footage and different angles of the fish, a practice considered unethical in the business of TV fishing shows.

By having a fish hooked for 25 minutes and fighting it hard three times, the fish undergoes a certain amount of stress. We'll never know how much, but one fishery biologist told me Dahlberg was increasing the potential harm to the fish by doing what he was doing.

When I spoke to Dahlberg, he admitted to letting the fish out three times and that it could have taken 25 minutes. But he said he allowed the fish to swim where it wanted on slack line so it could settle down. He said no pressure was placed on the fish during this time.

He actually claimed that what he was doing was helping the fish. The game wardens didn't agree. He was fined $250.

The episode is surprising because Dahlberg is known for being a staunch supporter of catch and release. He was even given the International Game Fish Association Award for Conservation.

"For me to be accused of molesting a fish is ironic," he told me.

Moronic might be the best word to describe two fishermen who stole a canoe and chained it to a large Ponderosa pine tree near Lake Mary in Flagstaff, Arizona. Jim Madden, a game warden for the Arizona Game and Fish, Region II, came across the freshly painted canoe, took down the hull identification number and discovered it was stolen.

So Madden went back and cut the lock and retrieved the canoe.

"On a whim, I stuck my business card on the tree," Madden says. "On the back of the card, I wrote: 'It's not safe to leave your boat out here, it will get vandalized or stolen. It is at our office for safe keeping, stop on by during business hours to pick it up. Sorry for any inconvenience this may cause. Jim Madden.'"

About two weeks later, the two thieves walked into the office and asked for their canoe. The anglers, two college students, were arrested and charged with theft and possession of stolen property. They were fined and put on unsupervised probation.

"If I recall correctly," Madden says, "one of them was a criminal justice major at Northern Arizona University."

Ouch.

With a myriad of fishing regulations, it stands to reason that even a few celebrities would bend a rule or two, mistakenly or not. Some are even caught red-handed (and red-faced) with their pants down.

CHRIS LeDOUX

Before becoming a country music sensation, Chris LeDoux was caught in an embarrassing pose: Fishing naked.

As a world champion rodeo star in the late 1970s, he was traveling from Rapid City, South Dakota, to Sidney, Nebraska.

One stop he made was in Bridgeport, Nebraska, to go swimming in an irrigation ditch.

"I happened to see this great big carp," LeDoux said. "We were borrowing somebody's pick-up and they had a fishing pole in the back. My friend was sitting under the shade trees. I'd been swimming in the nude, and found this fishing pole and decided I'll try to catch this fish. I told him, 'If you see anybody coming, like the game warden, holler so I can get rid of this pole.'

"Anyway, I killed a frog with a screwdriver along the bank, used it for bait and I was standing knee deep in the water fishing for this big carp, dangling this dead frog in front of him. Pretty soon, I heard my friend laugh in the background. 'Chris, turn around.'

"I couldn't hear him because of the water. This game warden pulled up right behind us. So there I was caught, naked, with a fishing pole. Anyway, he started reading me my rights. I said, 'Well, do you mind if I put my pants on first?' He said, 'Oh, yeah, go ahead.'"

LeDoux was taken downtown where he had to purchase a three-day fishing permit for $5 and pay a $10 fine.

"It ended up costing me $15, which was about all the money we had at the time," LeDoux says.

To borrow a phrase from his Grammy-nominated song, whatcha gonna do with a penniless, fishless cowboy, anyway?

DEION SANDERS

The story you are about to read is true. The names have *not* been changed to protect the innocent because, well, it was pretty much an open-and-shut case.

It involved Deion Sanders, a star in professional football and baseball. No question, he stood tall among his peers. But his stature shrank when it came to fishing a lake he wasn't supposed to fish. He discovered he was not above the law, though he apparently believed otherwise.

In the off season of 1996, Prime Time became a prime suspect for the repeated violation of fishing on private property in his hometown of Fort Myers, Florida. Sanders was in town for his charity basketball game.

Based on the arrest report from the Lee County Port Authority Police Department, the following is a re-enactment of Sanders's brush with the law.

May 7, 1996

It was 8:10 a.m. Deion Sanders and a friend were fishing for large-mouth bass at Lake No. 4 at the Southwest Florida International Airport when they were approached by patrolman James Mason.

Mason: "Fishing on airport property is not allowed, you're going to have to leave."

Sanders: "Why can't we fish here? We aren't bothering anyone."

Mason: "You're trespassing. Both of you are going to have to leave."

Sanders, continuing to cast: "We have to wait for our ride. Some friends took my truck to get some bait."

While the two anglers waited for their ride, Mason left the area, advised his supervisor of the situation and picked up another patrolman.

Upon returning to the lake, the patrolmen found Sanders and three others fishing.

Mason: "Listen, you guys can't be in the area, you have to leave. Nobody, not even airport employees are allowed to fish this area."

Sanders: "I know we're not supposed to be here, but there are some big bass in here."

The fish might have been biting, but the officers weren't. The fishing trip was over for Sanders and his friends.

Sanders: "I'll be back."

Mason: "You'll be subject to arrest if you return."

Sanders: "Y'all will just have to arrest me cause I'll be back tomorrow."

With that, Sanders and his fishing entourage departed.

May 9, 1996

It was 8:30 a.m. Officer Ralph Galietti and Sergeant Rick Severson responded to a call about two people fishing Lake No. 4. There, they found Deion Sanders and a friend with fishing rods in their hands getting ready to fish.

Galietti: "You'll have to leave the area. This is a no-trespassing area. You can't fish at the airport."

Sanders continued unloading other fishing gear while his friend listened attentively to the officer. Then Sanders took out a cell phone and started to make a call.

Sanders: "I'm calling my contact."

Galietti: "Hang up the phone, get your fishing gear packed up and leave the area."

Sanders: "Come on, I know people fish here."

Galietti: "I can either give you a written warning or arrest you for trespassing, what'll it be?"

Sanders: "I'll take the written warning."

Galietti wrote up the warning for unauthorized fishing and pointed out the no-trespassing signs to Sanders.

Then Sanders and his friend departed.

June 19, 1996

It was 7 p.m. Patrolman Dana Fox and Keith Francis noticed two males fishing from a small boat on Lake No. 4. As they got closer, Fox recognized one as being Deion Sanders. Fox knew Sanders had been warned twice before.

Fox: "How many times do you have to be warned about fishing in this area?"

Sanders: "I couldn't resist the temptation to come back and fish."

Fox asked Sanders several times to come ashore, but he continued to fish as if the officers were not there, catching a couple of bass in their presence. Fox advised Sanders that Sergeant Barry Merrill knew of the situation and was on his way.

Sanders: "I'll keep fishing until he gets here."

Fox again requested Sanders to come ashore.

Sanders: "You'll have to get the Coast Guard to get me off the lake."

Fox: "If I have to contact them, I'll have to impound your vehicle and boat, and put you in jail."

Sanders: "I've been to jail before. It doesn't scare me. I have a thousand people I could call to get me out."

Soon after this exchange, Sanders and his friend started toward shore. Sanders was getting ready to exit the boat when Sergeant Merrill and another patrolman arrived.

Merrill: "Haven't you received previous warnings about trespassing? Haven't you received a written warning?"

Sanders: "Yes, but I like to fish. I'm not doing anything wrong."

Merrill: "You're under arrest for trespassing after a warning."

Sanders became loud and aggressive, saying jail didn't scare him and all he needed to do was make one call and he'd be out.

After a "heated" discussion, Sanders was handcuffed and taken to the Lee County Port Authority in a patrol car. His friend was issued a trespass warning and sent off with Sanders's truck and unregistered boat.

Neither angler, incidentally, was in possession of a fishing license.

At the booking room, Sanders was cooperative and good-natured until it came time to sign the "notice to appear" form.

Booking photo of Deion Sanders.
Photo by Lee County Port Authority Police

Sanders: "I don't think I want to sign the notice. I want to go to jail."

Even after being told failure to sign would result in additional charges, he refused to sign. Not until after speaking several times with his attorney and meeting with a sergeant from the Fort Myers Police Department and with the Fort Myers police chief Larry Hart did Sanders finally sign.

He was then released, having been booked for the first-degree misdemeanor of trespassing.

"The only defense I have is that I'm sorry, but they were biting," Sanders told the *Fort Myers News-Press* that night. "I wasn't out there 10 minutes and they caught me. But I had 10 fish by that time.

"I truly have a passion for fishing. That airport is loaded with huge bass. Next time, I'm going out there in disguise."

June 20, 1996

It was a Thursday and Deion Sanders hosted a media gathering at his mother's house to promote his charity basketball game scheduled for the following night.

But basketball was a secondary topic. Instead, the press peppered him with moral questions, as reported in the *Fort Myers News-Press*.

Reporter: "Don't you think the trouble you got yourself into is not setting a good example for the kids who idolize you?"

Sanders: "I don't call that trouble. Jail's not a great thing. I don't glamorize it by any means . . . But I'm *fishing*. I'm *fishing*. I know you guys laughed. I was smiling."

Reporter: "What message does this send to kids by breaking the law?"

Sanders: "When you say 'breaking the law,' you've got to understand: Deion Sanders is not associated with drugs, alcohol, violence. I was fishing. It's the only way he relaxes in this world.

"I can't raise your kids. I have my own kids. I have two little kids. They know right from wrong."

The *News-Press* reported that Sanders alternated between admitting he was wrong and maintaining it was a crime he can somehow manage to live with.

Sanders: "They let Kent Hrbek and a lot of those guys who play for the Minnesota Twins—they let them out there all the time. But they don't let me. I guess it's 'cause I'm from Fort Myers."

Finally, someone asked him about the fish.

Sanders, smiling: "I got to keep the fish. I had a great time. Matter of fact, I just got done eating them at my grandmother's house."

Sanders avoided a first-degree misdemeanor charge that carries a $1,000 fine and up to a year in jail by striking a plea bargain.

Judge John Carlin ordered Sanders to pay $250 in fines and $130 in court costs, placed him on six-months' probation and ordered him to perform 50 hours of community service.

As for Sanders's charity basketball game? It just happened to be sponsored by the Fort Myers Police Department—an ironic twist, but not the only one.

Chief Hart told the News-Press *that Sanders had asked him about good places to fish as the two were organizing the charity game.*

Chief Hart: "I told him the best place to fish was the City Fish Market."

KEVIN SORBO

The statute of limitations ran out ages ago, so television star Kevin Sorbo, a.k.a. Hercules, unabashedly admits to breaking the law at Dutch Lake in his hometown of Mound, Minnesota.

He was 14 and he was fishing two weeks *before* the fishing season opened.

"I had a little Daredevil lure and I was casting off the shore," he recalls. "I pulled in a 15 1/2-pound northern pike. My parents wanted me to throw it back. But I said I can't, it's impossible for me to throw this thing back.

"Then walking home, you think everybody knows you did something illegal. I grew up pretty straight, with pretty strict parents. I think I wrapped it up in a bunch of leaves or something and smuggled it back to the house."

Sorbo wasn't too concerned, though.

"I did it more than once with largemouth bass and other fish," he says. "But that was a big one to pull out of a small lake like that. I was damned if I was going to throw the thing back."

PAUL BRANDT

The trophy trout was lying in the net on the bottom of the boat, and the Brandt family wondered if the law required the fish to be tossed back.

What was the fishing regulation? they wondered. Actually, it didn't much matter. Brandt's uncle had already reached the point of no return. The fish would be kept, fishing regulations be damned.

The episode occurred when Brandt was 16. He was fishing with his father and his uncle—"the fisherman of the family"—on Dixon Lake outside Calgary, where he grew up. The area is world renowned for its trout fishing.

But on this day, action was slow. They were without a bite until Paul hooked into something big.

"I figured it was something pretty good and I started reeling it in," the country music star recalls. "They weren't really paying any attention yet. Suddenly, they saw it jump and saw the rainbow color as it came out of the water.

"No quicker did that happen than my uncle had grabbed the rod from my hands and my dad jumped in the water with the net. We ended up pulling this thing out of there, and it was a 10-pound rainbow trout.

"It was funny because we didn't know what the size limits were and we were trying to figure it out. The manual was really quite confusing."

Normally, Brandt and his family practiced catch and release, but his uncle was adamant about keeping this trophy.

"So he throws it into a bag, we jump in the truck and take off," Brandt explains.

"Well, we found out later that if we had just kept the fish, brought it up to the ranger station, I would have had my name in the record books holding the fish with a picture in the local magazine and everything."

Nevertheless, the "undercover fishing operation" remains one of the great moments in Brandt's fishing career, a catch he says he'll never forget—even if it was taken from him.

Brandt remembers being upset at first, but his anger dissolved when he saw how big the fish was. He did tell them later that if he ever hooked something like that again, "don't even come near me."

RICK BARRY

Rick Barry doesn't know much about fishing, let alone fishing regulations, let alone fishing regulations in the backwoods of Alaska. So how was he to know a certain fish was out of season and illegal to catch?

Barry, a member of the NBA Hall of Fame, was in Anchorage for a golf event one summer when a group of 10 friends took a pair of seaplanes to a remote lake for a day of fishing.

"We went out and I caught this big old fish on one of the streams," Barry says. "The guy came back in the seaplane to pick us up and said, 'What you guys get?' I brought this fish over to show him. He said, 'You can't catch that fish, you'll get fined. That fish is out of season.' I said,

'What? I didn't know what kind of fish it is. I caught a fish, what do I know?'

"So I took the fish and threw it in the woods. He said, 'You're lucky the game warden didn't come by.'

"I don't know one fish from another. What do I know? I said, 'Hey, you guys needed to leave somebody up here who knew what they were doing. I don't know what I'm doing. I just throw it in there. If I catch something, I reel it in.'

"So I guess I left some food for the bears that night, but it was one of the biggest fish I ever caught and it was great. I didn't know what it was. I got rid of it quick, though, I'll tell you that.

"Actually, I felt very badly because the last thing I want to do is do something I'm not supposed to be doing. But it was kind of exciting to catch a fish that big."

Whatever it was.

Chapter Three

Sometimes Death Tugs at the Line

No doubt fishing is fun and exciting, whether pulling on a tiny bluegill or a behemoth bluefin tuna. It is generally considered to be risk free, unlike rock climbing without a rope (called solo climbing) or skydiving without a parachute (called fatal).

But fishing *can* be dangerous. It does have a dark side, however rare. I've written stories about a boat full of anglers capsizing in the frigid waters of an Eastern Sierra lake and rescuers arriving just before hypothermia. I wrote about two anglers who stood on the hull of their upside-down boat for 48 hours on the ocean before a sportfishing boat miraculously came by and rescued them.

Yes, an element of danger exists in fishing and sometimes it's more than just getting a hook accidentally embedded under your skin.

Sometimes the experiences are death defying, and in rare cases, believe it or not, a fish catches the fisherman. This might be funny if it weren't true.

It was the most incredible fishing story I've ever reported. An angler cheated death only because he often thought about the risk and possible consequences that his style of fishing presented.

John Whalen of Orange County, California, enjoys catching bluefin tuna the size of Volkswagen Bugs while using stand-up gear. He doesn't utilize a fighting chair, he just clips the rod and reel into the harness he wears around his waist and shoulders.

He also tightens the drag as much as he can to see how fast he can bring these monsters to the boat.

In March 1997, Whalen hooked into to a 350-pound bluefin off Cape Hatteras, North Carolina. His drag was tightened down. The boat dipped into a swell. The floor of the boat dropped out from under Whalen's feet, like a trapdoor being sprung. In a split second, he was pulled over the rail and taken hostage by the large tuna. He was helpless to escape, the harness acting like a straitjacket.

Whalen twisted in a spiral as the fish pulled him straight down into the deep, cold waters of the Atlantic.

Fortunately, he knew what to do. He had repeatedly envisioned an escape plan for this possibility:

Plan A: Try to unclip the rod. Plan B: Make sure to have a knife attached to you so you can cut the line. Plan C: Engage the reel's clicker and slowly back off the drag to prevent a backlash, then get to the surface.

As soon as he realized he was going overboard, Whalen took a quick breath. When he hit the water, he spread his legs to create drag, trying to slow or at least tire the fish.

Unclipping the rod from the harness was out of the question, unless the tuna decided to stop to allow him slack in the line. He didn't have a knife, so Plan B was out the window, too. One option remained: Engaging the clicker and backing off the drag slowly. If that didn't work, Whalen and the VW Bug would become inseparable. It would mean death by drowning.

Simply putting the reel into free spool would cause the line to unwind too fast, creating the tangled mess of a backlash or bird's nest. The spool would freeze in the tangle and line would stop unwinding. He would continue his one-way journey on the runaway freight train into the abyss.

But as if he had done it a thousand times, Whalen engaged the reel's clicker, backed off the drag and thumbed the reel as line slowly started to unwind. The death grip was easing.

Mark O'Brien, a friend who had jumped in after Whalen, heard the sound of the clicker underwater. It was sweet, comforting music. *John is still alive!*

As line peeled off the reel easier and easier, Whalen slowed to a stop, just as he had envisioned. He was close to 30 feet deep, he figures.

"Once I stopped, I needed air," he recalls.

With his left fingers and hand on the spool, Whalen used his right arm to swim to the surface where he exploded into fresh air and gulped in oxygen. O'Brien swam to Whalen and helped him to the boat. The others pulled him aboard.

A renowned billfish angler fishing on a boat nearby saw what happened and thought Whalen was a goner. Instead, Whalen escaped the unexpected death grip of the tuna as if he were Houdini.

"It all went so quickly," Whalen says. "If all that hadn't worked or if I would've gotten a bird's nest, I would not have had the air to do anything else. That was my one-shot deal. I would not have had the energy or strength to unclip myself and get out of my gear. It was an all-or-nothing deal."

The ordeal wasn't quite over, however. The fish was still on the line. The fight was not finished. The others put the harness back on Whalen and clipped the rod in. This time, a lifeline was attached, too, and the drag set not so tight. This time, Whalen was staying in the boat.

Almost out of instinct, he started reeling. Whalen, soaking wet and in shock, proceeded to reel the large tuna to the boat, then promptly released it as is customary in this catch-and-release fishery. The tuna and Whalen would live to fight again.

As the plane banked over Chesapeake Bay on the way home, O'Brien, sitting in a row behind Whalen, leaned over and patted the back of his seat.

"You know," he said. "I thought we were bringing you home in a box. Man, am I ever happy that you're sitting here."

A chill of realization ran through Whalen.

"I looked down at the bay and said, 'God, he's right. By all accounts, I should have been dead.'"

Sometimes danger lurks in the waters we fish. Sometimes death tugs at the line. Caution should not be tossed aside like old clothes. Whalen was lucky. So were these celebrities.

KEVIN COSTNER

The Perfect Storm, a best-selling book by Sebastian Junger, brought home a chilling recollection for actor Kevin Costner.

"We were in a storm like that," he recalls. "When I read that book, it just gave me shivers. ... I lived right through that."

One summer during his college days, Costner drove to the Northern California coast intent on getting a job on a commercial fishing boat.

An avid recreational angler, Costner was intrigued by the adventuresome stories told by an old salt about commercial fishing in Alaska.

Determined to discover his own adventure, he got a job on a boat based in Eureka, fishing for salmon and tuna.

One day, a storm came up and they were faced with a daunting decision: Make it easy and go with the storm but risk being delivered to San Francisco, far off the fishing grounds; or meet the storm head on and face the consequences.

To remain close to the fish, they chose to go into the storm. For more than 24 hours, Costner experienced life-threatening conditions as the boat crawled up the face of waves 40 to 50 feet high.

"We could have just gone down like a tank," he says.

At one point, the skipper turned the helm over to Costner in order to go below and get some sleep.

"If we'd have rolled, I'd have been dead," he says. "The water was ice cold. It was weird. To this day, I don't know if he actually went down and put on a dry suit and didn't tell me. I don't know if he had one on to protect himself if he had gone overboard.

"It was crazy."

Only after reading Junger's book did Costner realize how dangerous the experience had been and how fortunate he was to have survived his own perfect storm.

Kevin Costner sits in the bow of the commercial boat he worked on one summer during his college years. This was one of the calmer days. Costner survived his own "Perfect Storm" when his boat climbed walls of water 50 feet high.
Photo courtesy of Kevin Costner

CHUCK KNOX

Fishing isn't supposed to a life-threatening venture, though Chuck Knox could tell you otherwise.

The former NFL coach came within a couple of feet from getting shish kebab'd by a marlin while on an annual fishing trip with 40 players, coaches and friends in Cabo San Lucas, Mexico in 1974.

Knox, coach of the Los Angeles Rams at the time, was fishing with a friend, Howard Ashby, on a small boat with a skipper and deckhand.

Ashby had hooked up and was battling a marlin. When he got it to the boat, the skipper came down from the fly bridge to help the deckhand tag and release the fish.

Suddenly, another marlin leaped out of the water very close to the boat. To get a better view, Knox climbed two or three steps onto the ladder leading to the fly bridge.

What happened next took Knox's breath away.

"The marlin came out of the water and came across right through that fly bridge," Knox explains. "There's only a quarter of an inch of plywood up there. This fish knocked a big piece out of that board."

It then returned to the water, leaving on the surface a piece of evidence from the attack: A chunk of wood.

"We went and retrieved the piece of wood out of the water," Knox says. "There was a hole where the bill had gone through."

Later, the wood was made into a trophy perpetually given to the person catching the biggest marlin at the group's future gatherings. Fortunately, Knox was able to attend future gatherings.

"That fish missed me by maybe two feet," he says. "I'd have been a goner if that thing had hit me."

PICABO STREET

Picabo Street pulled the 135-pound halibut into the tiny Zodiac dinghy not knowing it could have been fatal.

As soon as the massive fish hit the rubber deck, it went ballistic, flopping around in the dinghy in an uncontrollable rampage.

Had Street been aware of the perils of catching large halibut in a small boat, she probably would have skipped this particular trip with her then-boyfriend, Mike Makar.

Street used to spend summers in Alaska where this story took place in 1994, before she earned fame in downhill skiing by winning silver and gold medals at the 1994 and 1998 Winter Games.

Makar shouted for Street to lift her legs off the dinghy's floor and hang them over the side to avoid getting chopped up by the halibut imitating a meat cleaver.

Pounding the fish over the head with a club was futile so Makar instructed Street to gaff the fish again.

"I'm like, 'Gaff it again? I'm going to put a hole in the boat!'" Street recalls.

"He's like, 'No, you gotta gaff it again, we gotta get it out of the boat. It's going to kill us.' So I had to gaff it again. Then we both lifted it up over the boat and I went to let it go and he's says, 'No, no, no, hang onto it! Hang onto it!'

"So I'm hanging on to it, it's flapping around, I'm leaning over the side of the Zodiac thinking we're all going into the drink, everything is going into the drink and then I hear this, 'click click.'"

Makar had loaded a shotgun. He told Street to hold the fish away from the boat then—boom!—shot a hole through its head.

"We finally got it into the boat, and we were completely covered with saltwater and halibut blood," Street says. "We were just trashed."

To calm the nerves, they broke open a bottle of Jack Daniels.

"Then he proceeded to tell me that they had found a guy the previous year in a Zodiac about the same size with a 150-pound halibut in the boat," Street says. "The man was found with a broken femur and he had bled to death."

GEORGE SEIFERT

NFL coach George Seifert and two friends were fishing for striped bass on the San Francisco coast in June 1987 when they noticed the overturned Boston Whaler. Sadly, three of the four anglers aboard had died four or five days before when their boat capsized.

"I remember us making the comment that they probably let their guard down and that you've got to pay attention more," Seifert recalls.

Twenty minutes later, Seifert and two of his fishing friends were wishing they had listened to their own words. They were fighting striped bass one moment and the next they were swimming for their lives.

"It was not a rough day," explains the Super Bowl-winning coach of the 1989 and 1994 San Francisco 49ers. "We all heard about sneaker waves. We looked up and the bow of the boat was pointing out to sea. Then a wave hit us and actually flipped us all out of the boat."

The anglers, each of them busy reeling in striped bass, didn't notice the boat drifting from beyond the breakwater right into it. A wave hit bow first and flipped the boat upside-down.

"I remember the boat kind of pushing me under the water, actually the pressure pushing me to the sand," Seifert recalls. "We were not in deep water obviously."

As if coaching a close football game, Seifert remained calm. He did not panic. He conjured images from when he was a kid body-surfing and tumbling in the same surf. It was just like wiping out. He felt at home.

But a funny thing happened when Seifert reached the surface.

"All of a sudden, I saw a 25-pound striper floating in front of me," he says. "I damn near hit it with my face.

"I had rain pants on and they were going down over my knees so I couldn't swim. But I wanted to try to bring the striped bass in, so I had to make a choice. Obviously, I chose life and I dove under the water and took the rain pants off and swam to the beach and lost the fish."

For an instant, Seifert had grasped the large striped bass that he had caught earlier in the day. Letting go was his only option. The fish was lost, as was the rest of their catch. Their gear was lost, too, and the boat totaled. But their lives were spared.

Over the years, Seifert and his friends haven't talked much about this ill-fated trip. Seifert says it's because you don't talk about things where you demonstrate your ineptness.

At least Seifert can glean some humor from the tragedy. After all, the one that got away is like none other.

"I laugh at it now because that should've been the last thing I was thinking about was getting that fish in," he explains.

"But it was like, 'Dog-gone it, we're going through all this, it sure would be nice to get this fish in.'"

Chapter Four

Fishing Follies

J ust as you never know when a fish will bite, one cannot anticipate when Mother Nature's curtain might rise to unveil a comedic performance on her stage, something along the lines of a Vaudeville routine.

The gag is unexpected, but that's a large part of what fishing is about. You never know what might happen next. It begins with something out of the ordinary, a mishap, a whoops-a-daisy, a did-that-just-really-happen? type of incident. It often ends with everyone in stitches—either sutures or the split-a-gut variety.

In fishing, as in every day life, stuff happens.

A fish jumps into the boat. A fish jumps into the boat and hits you on the noggin or bites you. A cow falls from the sky and sinks your boat—yes, a cow! A lure gets snagged in your ear or hand or chin. *Ouch.* OK, so that would only be funny if it isn't you.

Really, there's no limit to the amount of laughs a fishing trip can produce.

One of the most hilarious fish stories I've reported on landed on *America's Funniest Home Videos.* It gave credence to the old adage about fishing being so good the fish were jumping into the boat.

Scott Spiro was fighting a 265-pound striped marlin aboard a charter boat off Cabo San Lucas. His wife, Patsy, was videotaping the battle. As he reeled the fish closer to the boat, Scott urged his children, Jonathan and Nicholas, nine and seven at the time, to come to the rail to get a closer look at the gorgeous creature.

Suddenly, the marlin leaped high out of the water parallel to the stern and back into the water. Someone standing at the stern could have reached out and touched the fish it was that close. An instant later, in the starboard corner, the fish did an abrupt u-turn and came straight up out of the water and *into the boat!*

The marlin went ballistic, thrashing about on the deck in a vain attempt to escape this foreign place he accidently fell into. Rods and reels went flying as the fish contorted its body back and forth, swinging its dangerous sword. Spiro retreated into the cabin with his wife and kids, seeking refuge. Patsy kept filming as the two crew members attempted to subdue the fish.

Jonathan and Nicholas are clearly heard laughing hysterically in the background on the videotape. They were getting a real kick out of this unusual show. Fortunately, everybody could laugh about it since nobody got hurt, except for the marlin. And the boat.

Once the fish was dead, the crew surveyed the damage. The deck looked like a hurricane had struck. Immediately the crew noticed that one of the two fighting chairs that were permanently fixed to the deck was missing. As the fish was doing its slam dance, it had dislodged the chair from its pedestal and tossed it into the water as easily as dropping a marlin jig overboard.

"The captain was scared he was going to lose his job," Scott said. "He had to explain to the owner of the boat where this fishing chair went. He wanted me to show the video to prove what happened."

Back on land, they did just that. The Spiro family also showed the videotape over and over to people aboard the cruise ship they were on, becoming celebrities of sorts.

"We tell people we have quite a fish tale," Patsy said. "It was pretty exciting for our very first marlin."

Another story involving fish jumping into boats comes from the Mississippi and Missouri rivers. Talk about incredible.

So many fish are jumping into boats, fishermen and other boaters must defend themselves with some sort of protection device lest they become broken-nose victims of the flying silver carp from Asia.

The flying fish are so prevalent, one fisherman was videotaped holding up a frying pan and catching a carp in it. This tape also made *America's Funniest Home Videos.*

The phenomena of flying carp has been documented on *CBS News with Dan Rather* and CBS' *Inside Edition*, along with a variety of other TV shows.

"You just have to see it to believe it," said Danny Brown, fisheries management biologist for the Missouri Department of Conservation in St. Louis.

"They've hit several of us and haven't severely injured any of us, but there's all kinds of war stories going around about people getting their noses broken."

You never know when you'll get sucker punched, either, since they come flying in from all angles.

Silver carp are known to jump six to eight feet out of the water year-round, but the jumping is more pronounced during warm-water months. Why they jump is unclear. The prevailing explanation is that the vibration from approaching boat motors stir them into a jumping frenzy.

The average size of the jumpers are 12 to 15 pounds. No wonder fishermen and boaters are taking cover.

"I tell people that anything that can be damaged by a thrown bowling ball can be damaged by a flying carp," said Duane Chapman, fisheries biologist of the Columbia Environmental Research Center in Columbia, Missouri. "If you're doing 20 mph and one of these things jumps into your boat, it breaks things. It could be your neck or your fishing rod or your girlfriend.

"Sometimes they jump up and hit the throttle mechanism. You can imagine what it's like to all of a sudden unexpectedly floor your boat."

Which is why protective netting was put up in Chapman's research boat and why many boaters arm themselves with other CDDs—Carp Deflection Devices—as Chapman jokingly refers to them.

Some people carry metal trash-can lids. Some hide behind lawn chairs. Some try catching them out of midair with big landing nets. Some have even found carp to be ideal clay targets, illegally using a shotgun to shoot them out of the air.

"Every pleasure boater you see is in some way dealing with these fish," Chapman said.

It's like speeding through a shooting gallery, hoping you don't get hit.

"We had 14 jump into our boat one day," Brown said. "We were out no more than two hours. It's just constant."

The carp eat algae and zooplankton, so they were stocked into catfish hatcheries in Missouri and Arkansas to keep the ponds clean. They are said to have been introduced into the river systems during the 1993 floods. Since then, they have been multiplying.

Now, biologists are working on a means of controlling the flying bowling balls.

"It's not as funny as it used to be, because there are so many of them," Brown said. "We're all just waiting to get our nose broke now."

Who'd have ever thought hard hats would be a required part of your fishing tackle?

Hard hats would have been a wise choice for the commercial fishermen aboard a trawler working the waters of the Sea of Japan one spring in the late 1990s.

A cow fell from the sky, hit the trawler and sank it. Udderly ridiculous? No, it's true. Crew members lived to tell about it. But authorities apparently felt that to believe them would be to believe the cow was returning to earth after having jumped over the moon. So the crew reportedly was held on suspicion of sabotage until Russian authorities came forward to confirm it really did occur.

Seems a Russian air force crew member stole the cow from near the landing strip and stowed it in the cargo hold of the plane. While flying over the Sea of Japan, the beast went berserk. Perhaps it was upset at the choice of in-flight movies or the food. For whatever reason, the cow was uncontrollable. The crew decided to unload its unruly cargo by opening the door and shoving it out. Little did they know they were unleashing a deadly cow bomb.

One of the earliest fishing tales occurred off Catalina Island in the early 1900s when boatman Jim Gardner was seen getting repeatedly pulled under water after his small boat capsized. Everyone who saw it suspected he was getting attacked by sharks.

Charles Holder, the founder of the Avalon Tuna Club at Catalina off Southern California, had boated a 100-pound tuna. Suddenly, the fish came alive and the anglers scrambled to one side of the boat, causing it to overturn.

The fish was lost, the gear was lost and one of the anglers who couldn't swim almost was lost. Another boat nearby motored over to rescue the anglers and that's when they saw Gardner, presumably trying to fight off sharks.

"They're all just panicking," says Michael Farrior, the Tuna Club historian. "He gets near the boat and pops up out of the water and said, 'Hello sir, I've got your fish.'"

Gardner still had a hold of the gaff and the still-fighting fish. With relief, they pulled him and the fish on board. As the boat started to motor to shore, Gardner felt a sharp sting in his leg. It was a hook. It was the hook at the end of the line of Holder's rod and reel. The outfit was pulled up. It wasn't lost after all.

Not a day goes by without something bizarre happening in the world of fishing, or so it seems. I've come across countless other tales: Alaskan anglers hooking up to whales, an angler losing his car into a lake after forgetting to set the parking brake, an angler finding a cellphone in the stomach of the cod he caught, salmon and trout jumping into boats, barracuda and tiger muskie jumping into boats and biting anglers, fish pulling fishing rods overboard and then getting caught by someone else, who pulls up the lost rod and reel, a lake angler hooking something that turns out to be a wedding dress. Wacky and wonderful, no?

One episode of *Inside Sportfishing* showed an angler hooked up to a thresher shark while fishing from a kayak. As the shark pulled the angler out to sea, the angler crossed the line of another kayak fisherman. The angler dropped his rod and reel in the water as he frantically tried to clear the line and the dangerous hooks heading his way. An instant later, the angler had a pierced chin, from which hung a perfectly placed Rapala lure.

"The hook was stuck in the bone," said *Inside Sportfishing* host Michael Fowlkes. "So the guy took a pair of side cutters and after several tries, was able to cut the hook in half, leaving only the stud sticking out of his chin. He borrowed another outfit and kept fishing."

Later that night, the angler went to the emergency room to have the hook removed.

Not everybody receives body piercing from a fish, or has a fish jump into their boat, or has a cow fall *through* their boat. But almost assuredly everyone has a fishing moment full of chuckles.

One of mine occurred on a Southern California lake when my stepdaughter, Ericka Slaten, went to set the hook on a tiny crappie, rearing back hard on the rod as if trying to set the hook on a huge tuna. Only it wasn't a huge tuna. It wasn't even a tiny crappie. It was a snag. The line snapped and down she went, behind landing with a thud in the bottom of the boat. A laugh track could've been recorded on the resulting reaction from Ericka and my wife, Cindy, and the rest of us who saw the show.

Another Keystone Cops episode occurred while fishing with my parents in Alaska. I accidentally knocked a salmon off my mom's hook with the net, but the fish must have been stunned. My dad asked for the net, backed up the boat and netted the free-swimming fish that didn't get away.

One time while harbor fishing in a small skiff with my folks, I was reeling in a bonito on light tackle. The fish was eager to get into the boat and I easily swung it over the rail, hitting my mom in the chest. We found out why the fish was in a hurry to climb aboard. It was being chased by a California sea lion, which came over the rail and nearly climbed into the boat, too. He finally sunk into the water—without our bonito.

We've shared a few guffaws over those tales through the years. We've also laughed with pride over the million times mom has out-fished us all or caught the biggest fish.

Another time, my brother Leonard and I were fishing for trout on an Arizona lake and found an unorthodox method of getting the fish to bite. If we stood up the hill 30 feet away from our fishing rods, the trout would strike our baits. Amazingly, it would only work if we stood on the hill. With every bite, our laughter echoed across the lake.

On that same trip, as darkness fast approached, we piled four fishermen and all the gear into a two-man canoe and cautiously paddled a mile across the lake back to our car. The water line was maybe two inches from the top of the canoe. If someone sneezed, we were doomed. It was as though we were walking a tightrope as a group.

Fortunately, we didn't lose our balance and nobody sneezed, and a cow didn't fall out of the sky and sink us.

VINCE GILL

Vince Gill was hoping something would bite, though not something with four legs and a tail, not to mention a bark. But that's what happened. By accident, Gill became a dogcatcher.

The country music star was fishing the waterways in Miami Beach, Florida, in 1979, taking a break from cutting an album.

He was walking through a neighborhood making casts along the docks. Gill noticed one across the waterway with a big pylon and he felt certain it held a big bass. So he began casting toward it.

On a nearby lawn, a dog barked at him, but he paid it no attention. At least not until he accidentally sent a cast over the water, over the dock and onto the yard with the barking dog.

"This dog saw the lure and took off from the deck and ran," Gill recalls. "I was reeling as fast as I humanly could, but I didn't get it reeled in in time and the dog pounced on this lure."

The treble hooks dug into the dog. When it took off running, the line tightened and started peeling off the reel, as if Gill had hooked a large fish. *Zzzzz.*

"Then I hear this howling, crying, barking dog that's going nuts," Gill says. "He finally bit the line off. Now I'm thinking I've got to go tell these people what I've done."

When he approached the house, a sign greeted him: Beware of Dog. An older woman in curlers and a house robe answered the door.

"Ma'am, you're not going to believe this," Gill started, "but I have just hooked your dog with a fishing lure. You've got to find your dog, he's hurt."

Suddenly, from around the house, the dog raced toward Gill with a Cujo-like attitude.

"The dog leaps at me, bites me in the leg, I've got blood running down my leg and this lady is going, 'Oh my God, now you're going to sue me.'"

Gill assured the lady he wouldn't sue her. For despite his bloody wound, Gill felt much worse for the dog.

"The lure was hung in the poor dog's crotch."

SAMUEL L. JACKSON

If it were a movie, this fishing adventure starring actor Samuel L. Jackson might have been called *Clueless in Seattle*.

On tour in Seattle for the play *A Soldier's Story* in his early days, Jackson and three friends took a break to rent a boat and go salmon fishing in Puget Sound.

The inexperienced anglers picked a spot and started fishing, drinking beer, laughing, talking, hanging out. And drifting.

Soon, their landmark disappeared. As they wondered where they were, they noticed in the distance an oil tanker as big as a New York City block. They ignored it and kept fishing.

A few minutes later, they spotted something dark quickly approaching.

"We didn't know anything about wakes," Jackson explains. "This wake comes by and we're on the top of it. Then the water drops from under us and the boat, drops like 20 feet—boom!—to the bottom. We fire up the motor, we're like 'vvvrt, vvvrt, vvvrt,' trying to get out of there.

"Next thing we know, another wake comes and again we go up with it. All of a sudden, the boat stays with the wake and the boat's gone, and we're all in the air looking down at the boat like 20 feet to the left of us. We're like 'Ahhhhhh.'

"It's the funniest thing in the world. The time it took for us to go from 10, 15 feet in the air and come down, the boat came back in seconds and we hit right into the boat. It was so incredible.

"And we never got wet, never got wet. Then we got the motor fired up and jetted out of there."

They found calmer waters and continued fishing long enough for Jackson to catch a salmon. Later, they returned to port, feeling grateful for getting back to land safe from the Sound.

"We had a huge laugh afterward, but it wasn't until we got back to shore that we realized, 'Hmmm, we could've been in a spot of trouble out there.'"

GARRY MARSHALL

Garry Marshall used to enjoy taking his son, Scott, fishing on the Santa Monica Pier in Southern California. It was a nice escape from the rigors of his career as an actor, director, producer and writer.

But the man known for producing *The Odd Couple*, *Laverne and Shirley* and *Happy Days* couldn't escape an aspiring writer, who trespassed on his privacy.

Marshall and his then seven-year-old son were fishing on the pier one day during the height of his Hall of Fame TV career.

"It was getting cold, so I said, 'You stay here, Scotty, and I'll go back and get you a jacket,'" Marshall says. "So I went back to the car and when I came back, he was holding a script. He said, 'Some man gave me a script he said to give to you.'"

Marshall shook his head.

"They won't even let us fish!!!"

To say Marshall didn't like his fishing interrupted is an understatement. The script might as well have become fish wrap. Needless to say, it went unread.

"I sent the script back," Marshall says, laughing. "I said, 'I cannot read when I fish.'"

MARK O'MEARA

Tiger Woods can drive a golf ball 300 yards. Ask him to make a cast with a baitcasting outfit and he might need several mulligans, like any other amateur bass angler.

PGA star and veteran bass fisherman Mark O'Meara learned this firsthand when he took Woods bass fishing on the Butler chain of lakes in Orlando, Florida soon after Tiger turned golf professional.

"Do you bass fish?" O'Meara asked.

"I love to bass fish," Woods replied.

"All right. Can you throw a baitcasting reel?" O'Meara asked.

"Oh yeah, yeah," Woods replied.

So O'Meara handed Woods a baitcasting rod and reel, a dangerous outfit in the hand of a beginner because backlashes occur when you forget to thumb the reel when casting. The resultant tangle of line is called a bird's nest.

"It was kind of windy and we got on some fish that were rising to the surface, chasing some bait," O'Meara recalls. "His first cast—whoosh—major bird's nest. He said, 'Well, it's been a while.' I said, 'Yeah, and it's going to take you a while to unravel that nest you got in that reel.'

"He tried for a while and then I said, 'You know what, forget it. Just throw that one down. I got another rod over there. I've got a spinning rod you can throw. It's fool proof.'"

Like his golf game, Woods has since improved his fishing technique and has even picked up fly fishing, but clearly he double-bogeyed the first trip with O'Meara.

"The moral to the story is, he can bring his own fishing rod next time," O'Meara concludes. "It took me 30 minutes to fix the one he messed up."

RICK RHODEN

As a pitcher in Major League Baseball for 15 years, Rick Rhoden knew all about getting the hook, the baseball vernacular for a pitcher being pulled from a game.

Getting the hook in fishing has a completely different connotation. A rather painful one, as Rhoden found out.

Rhoden was living on a golf course. He not only golfed the course but fished it, too. One day in 1993 he was fishing the course when he got his hooks into a bass and vice versa.

"I was at a pond about half a mile from the house and I was catching some bass," he says. "I had a little topwater plug and caught about a one-pound bass. I was taking the hooks out and it kicked and embedded a hook in my finger. I couldn't get it out of its mouth because he had two treble hooks in there and I had one in my finger. So I went home carrying the fish on my hand."

At home, his wife, Liz, was at a loss.

"She didn't know what to do," he says. "When I told her to cut the head off, she was afraid she was going to cut my finger."

But Liz managed to cut the fish's head off without further incident.

"So I went to the emergency room with a fish hook and a fish head in my hand," Rhoden says. "I got to the hospital and the doctor took wire clippers and clipped the plug off so it was just the hooks. Then he gave me a shot in the finger and kinda ripped the hook out.

"The nurses at the emergency room thought it was pretty funny.

"It was comical at the time, but it didn't feel too comical. I was just glad I was close to home. I'm glad I wasn't 30 miles out in the woods somewhere."

NEAL McCOY

One of Neal McCoy's best friends is NBA star Karl Malone, whose goal in life was to meet Hall of Fame pitcher, and fellow fisherman, Nolan Ryan.

Since McCoy is also Ryan's friend, the country music star hooked the two of them up for a fishing outing. It was summer of 1997, sometime after Malone's Jazz reached the NBA finals.

"We all finally found a day off," McCoy said.

So McCoy and Malone flew down to meet Ryan at Laguna Madre off the coast of Texas where they would target red fish.

"It was for one of Nolan's TV fishing shows, but we didn't catch much," McCoy said. "I hadn't fished in 20 years and I out-caught both of them. I think Nolan caught two, Karl caught one and I caught four. It was just one of those bad days."

Particularly for Malone.

"Karl and I had never wade fished," McCoy explained. "We were wading in the lagoon. It's the ocean. It was waist high to me and knee high to Karl. As soon as the boat stopped, Nolan takes off walking and the guide takes off walking. Karl and I, we haven't seen each other for a while so we're walking around, casting and shooting the bull. Then he got stung by a jellyfish.

"That was the end of it. He was mad, too. He started cussing. I said, 'You're on TV, you're miked.' He said, 'I don't give a...' He just went off. He cussed for about 30 minutes. Believe me, they didn't get much out of the program, but we sure had a lot of fun."

CHRISTOPHER ATKINS

Christopher Atkins of *Blue Lagoon* movie fame and renown for his role on television's *Dallas*, likes to get away by himself to fish.

So one winter afternoon, off he went, pedaling his mountain bike into the canyon of Malibu Creek State Park near Los Angeles, heading for a fishing hole in search of a big largemouth bass.

Atkins fought through the thicket far from the trail to reach a pool in the creek that he felt certain held a big fish.

"Now the adrenaline is pumping and it's starting to get cold," he recalls. "I flicked my lure out there, but I missed my target and snagged a stick. It was one of those that when you pull it, the stick comes, but it wouldn't come far enough to reach it. So I'm leaning over trying to get this thing. I'm leaning over and leaning over and leaning over and reeling in and reeling in. The lure was right at my fingertips...and the bank gives way.

"I was standing about three feet off the water and the dirt bank slid out from under my feet. I ended up in the creek up over my head."

But that wasn't the worst part about it, he says.

Atkins quickly climbed out, lucky to get up the slippery embankment without any help. He was in the middle of nowhere, it was getting dark, he was soaking wet and he was starting to shiver.

But that wasn't the worst part about it, either, he says.

He loaded up his bike and started back to his car, two miles away, the cold wind giving him concern about hypothermia.

"I was so cold I couldn't stop shaking and couldn't move my hands off the bar of the bicycle," he says. "I finally got back to the car and was soaking wet. Even that wasn't the worst part about it.

"The worst part about it was when I finally got home and got out of the car and I came in the house and all you heard was 'Squeak, squeak, squeak,' from all the water in my shoes and I was frozen to death...

"My wife busted a gut.

"'Ah-ha-ha-ha-ha-ha-ha, ah-ha-ha-ha-ha-ha-ha, what happened to you?' Here I was, 'I'm going to go fishing for a little while, honey,' and I come home and I'm soaked.

"Now when I go fishing, she asks if I'm taking my swimsuit and starts laughing. It's a true story. To this day she gives me grief."

Actor Christopher Atkins holds a trophy largemouth bass. Atkins is the maker of his own lures through his company www.rockyriveroutdoors.com.
Photo courtesy of Christopher Atkins

JOHN MICHAEL MONTGOMERY

Not long after his country music debut, before making it big, singer John Michael Montgomery used financial caution when purchasing a fishing boat in 1993.

A few years before, a boat he owned was repossessed because he couldn't pay for it. So he found a used, one-man boat and bought it for $100—or about what it was worth.

The first time out on Harrington Lake in Kentucky, his brother, Eddie, and a friend motored up to him to chat.

"Man, you know since we've been talking it looks like that boat's getting lower and lower in the water," Eddie said. "You might want to jump into my boat."

John's boat was sinking. He figured he could get it back to the dock but soon realized he needed to abandon ship.

"That thing had a crack in it or something," John said. "By the time I got it about halfway back, the whole nose was under the water and it was going under."

Eddie came to the rescue. John joined him, and they towed the piece of junk back to shore. Fortunately his brother was nearby.

"If my brother hadn't been out there that afternoon, there ain't no telling what would've happened," John said. "I'd have been all right, but it wouldn't have been any fun, I'll tell you that."

Chapter Five

Something Smells Fishy

The Edgewater Inn was built in 1962 on Puget Sound in Seattle and used to be the only hotel where one would request a "fishing" or "non-fishing" room.

In the old days, hotel guests would fish out of the windows. Seriously. In the lobby gift shop, rods and reels were rented and bait purchased.

"Can I help you?"

"Yes, I'd like a newspaper, toothpaste, some antacids and a package of frozen herring, please."

In the privacy of their rooms, guests would open their windows to a whole new concept in fishing.

If you weren't going to fish, you certainly didn't want a room where it was allowed. One can imagine the carpet soaking up the juices from the bait or whatever fish were caught. Presumably, an unpleasant odor lingered for the next guest much like the smells of cigarette smoke are left behind by a smoker.

Not only did guests actually catch fish, they often cleaned them in their rooms, too.

Yuck.

George Washington never slept and fished at the Edgewater, but the Beatles did during their 1964 American tour. So did rock star Frank Zappa, who eventually sang about the mud sharks he caught from a window at the Edgewater.

"Mud sh-sh-shark.

"We're gonna do a little dancing,

"A little dancing thing called the Mud Shark.

"Now, this dance started up in Seattle..."

Mudsharks or cod were typical catches. If the cod was big enough, the hotel chef would prepare it for you for dinner. The catch of the day was never fresher.

American League umpires working games in Seattle used to stay at the fishing hotel and were said to have partook of this unusual activity. One even came up with an ingenious method to ensure he never missed a bite—even when he was at the hotel bar.

It's a classic tale. He tossed his bait into the water and tied the line around the telephone receiver. He replaced the receiver to its cradle and then went to the downstairs bar for a drink.

Every so often he'd sidle up to the house phone in the bar and called his room. If the line rang and rang, he knew he needed to be patient and give it a little more time.

"Uh, bartender, another cold one, please! The fish just aren't biting."

But if the line was busy, he knew he had hooked a fish because it had pulled the receiver off its cradle.

"Excuse me, gotta run. I've got a hook-up."

He'd chug down his cold one and race up to his room to reel in his catch, whatever it might be.

New meaning was given to the phrase "I've got a fish on the line." What would Alexander Graham Bell have thought?

The new hotel owners put a halt to window fishing sometime in the 1980s, probably figuring it'd be best to clean up this messy act and force anglers to fish in more traditional spots. Like from a boat or pier, even though the hotel was built on a pier—Pier 67.

Whether it's bait mashed into the carpet of a hotel room or fish-smelling hands wiped on your pants or putrid catfish bait or plain ol' fish just smelling fishy—incidentally, is that an oxymoron, fish smelling fishy?—one thing is a given in fishing: It can stink.

In some form or fashion, fishing produces a myriad of pungent aromas that fill the nostrils and can diminish your appetite for fish that don't taste fishy.

Of course, sometimes, "fresh fish" is in the nose of the beholder.

The salmon a friend caught from the Sacramento River one summer in the early 1970s was definitely fresh when he landed it, but not so fresh when he got it home. He stopped by Conlin Bros. Sporting Goods where my father and I worked to show off his catch. When we got to his car, we expected to see the fish laying on a bed of ice in a cooler.

Instead, the 15-pound salmon sat in the bottom of his trunk wrapped in a blanket like a baby. The eyes were glazed over with # signs. The once, bright silvery skin looked dull and dry, as if it had sat in a hot trunk for 10 hours without being put on ice. And no wonder, it *had* sat in a hot trunk for 10 hours without being put on ice. He had driven from Sacramento to Los Angeles with the salmon cooking in the trunk. The smelly fish and trunk were something only a swarm of flies could love.

The catfish angler, probably more than any other fisherman, puts up with more disgusting scents while fishing than a hound dog detects on an afternoon walk.

Just the smell of the various stink baits you use to catch catfish is enough to make you prefer fishing for bass or bluegill. My father-in-law, Frank Morkes, a veteran farm-pond fisherman in Oklahoma, loves to fish for catfish. Each year a friend of his makes up a batch of dip bait. The recipe calls for something like two cans of sardines, two jars of garlic, a pound of cheese and a pound of cow brains from the local slaughterhouse. You didn't even have to smell it, just thinking about it made you want to gag.

Hog Wild is a popular commercial stink bait for catfish. Just don't get it on your clothes. Otherwise, plan on discarding them at the end of the day. The stink is 100 percent, pure raunchy. Tackle shops place signs near the bait, warning anglers not to open the jar in the store.

What happens if they do? My father, the store manager, found out one morning when an employee with a sense of humor—and no fear of termination—opened a jar of the reeking catfish bait and left it hidden overnight in the camping section. No sleeping bags or tents were sold the next day.

The anglers pursuing catfish in the Mississippi and Missouri river systems must contend with more than just smelly bait. They must avoid getting slimed.

Asian carp are the skunks of fish. The silver carp leaves a distinct calling card and delivers it by airmail. These things jump six to eight feet out of the water, apparently prompted by the sound of approaching boat motors.

Problem is, they're jumping into boats. A plastic poncho and hard hat are recommended.

"When they hit you, they leave a coating of blood and slime on you," said Danny Brown, fisheries management biologist for the Missouri Department of Conservation. "It's just unbelievable. You can't just wash it off.

"It's like glue, and they bleed profusely. The second they get in your boat, they start to bleed out of their scales all over their body. There's just blood everywhere, and mucus, bloody slime. That's why you hate getting hit by the things. The smell—they're very smelly."

Not only that, the silver carp's head apparently isn't made for sudden impacts. When they hit something, sometimes their heads will fly off their bodies. Yeesh. Kind of makes you want to take up bowling. Then again, if you must rent shoes, a certain smell persists in bowling, too.

Not all fishing smells are repulsive. Some aromas make the whole fishing adventure worthwhile.

For instance, anglers yearn for the smell of a just-caught trout cooking over a campfire. A fresh salmon being hickory-smoked along an Alaskan river. The scent of pine trees surrounding a mountain lake or stream. The distinct smell of largemouth bass on your fingers signifying a successful day of catching and releasing.

But the most delightful smell of all, the clear-your-nostrils variety anglers hope to find every time out?

Fresh air.

JAY LENO

Jay Leno never cared much for fishing. He calls it a nap with a stick. *The Tonight Show* host was into cars and motorcycles, yet his father wanted him to do something outdoorsy.

"Why don't you take up something like fishing?" he asked his son, and then went out and bought him a fishing rod. But Jay didn't want to go fishing.

Even his mother prodded him to give it a try for his father's sake. Still, Jay refused.

"Then I was in school one day," Leno recalls, "and was talking with a buddy of mine and he said, 'You know the lake by my house? They're draining it.' I said, 'Oh?' He says, 'Yeah, there's tons of dead fish in this lake.'

"'There are?'

"So I ride my bike over there and we scoop up all these dead fish, about 30 of them. I put them all on a stringer and everything and I come in and go, 'Hey dad, I went fishing today. Look what I caught!'

"My father just beamed with pride. 'Hey, look at all the fish my boy caught! I knew you could do it.'"

Meanwhile, his mother took the fish into the kitchen to clean and get them ready to cook. As soon as she did, she began to gag. The fish smelled horrible. They couldn't be eaten. She asked where Jay got them.

"I confessed under threat of frying pan," he says. "'OK, I scooped them up from the lake they've been draining. They've been dead for a while.' My mother got all upset and threw all the fish out. But so as not to disappoint my father, she went to the store and bought some fresh fish."

That night, the Leno household ate fish for dinner. It wasn't until a couple of weeks later that Jay's father learned the truth.

"He said something like, 'Oh for goodness sakes, what the hell kind of stupid thing is that to do?' That was pretty much the extent of my fishing."

PAT O'BRIEN

Just after college, Pat O'Brien and some college buddies would vacation on Nantucket Island, where each year they ate bluefish until they were blue in the face.

With virtually no money, they'd rent some fishing gear on the first day and catch as many bluefish as they could.

"Then for the next three weeks, that's all we would eat is bluefish," the host of *The Insider* remembers.

"Bluefish for breakfast, bluefish for lunch, bluefish for dinner. Poached bluefish. Fried bluefish. Bluefish *tartare*. Grilled bluefish. Bluefish and bread. Bluefish soup.

"To this day, I like catching them, but I can't throw them back quick enough."

NATHANIEL CROSBY

Nathaniel Crosby was on the University of Miami golf team when he turned his old Chevy van into an oven and cooked some trout.

In the late 1970s, the son of the late Bing Crosby was invited to play Juniper Hills Golf Club and afterward went fishing with old golfer Julius Boros and George Low.

He caught a couple of trout and put them in a Styrofoam box filled with ice.

"The next week, I was off to play a golf tournament with the college team and left that box in the van for the whole week, parked at my apartment," Crosby says. "Miami gets pretty hot, so..."

So you can imagine what greeted Crosby when he opened the van door upon his return.

"It was nasty, nasty stuff," he says. "The smell never left the van. That van, hopefully, has been destroyed by now. If it's still around, I'll guarantee it still smells."

RUSH LIMBAUGH

Political commentator Rush Limbaugh has no desire to become a fisherman. He tried it and did not like it.

"As a kid I caught 18 bluegill in an afternoon of fishing in a river in Illinois," he explains. "My parents made me clean the fish. I didn't get the smell off my hands for about a week. Never again, that was it.

"I still have no interest in fishing."

KIM ALEXIS

Tradition calls for an angler to be tossed into the harbor by the boat's crew to celebrate the catching of his or her first billfish. Supermodels are not exempt.

Supermodel Kim Alexis caught her first billfish and won a marlin tournament in Cancun, Mexico with a 125-pound blue marlin.

It took her only 15 minutes to land, enough time for her to experience numbing in her arms and hands. Boy, was she happy to uncurl her fingers afterward. She wasn't as thrilled with the boat's crew following tradition and tossing her into the harbor.

"It was disgusting," she says. "They sort of just grabbed me and threw me in. It was filled with all that blood and guts and all the stuff from where they were cleaning fish. Yuck."

Kim's father was a fisherman, but she doesn't consider herself an avid angler, and not because of the unexpected dunking.

"No," she says, "I get seasick and queasy out there, so I'm much happier on land."

DON SHULA

Long before Don Shula diagramed Xs and Os and became one of the all-time great NFL coaches, he worked as a fisherman.

"I learned how to fillet fish at an early age," he says. "I learned all about the fishing industry."

What was the catch? His father was a commercial fisherman.

As a teenager, Shula worked part-time in a fish house on the shores of Lake Erie, where commercial boats would haul in pike, perch and pickerel by the tons. Shula helped net fish, fillet fish, pack fish, ice down fish and store fish.

"I got to see a lot of fish in my youth," Shula says.

So when he became coach of the Miami Dolphins, it was a natural fit, right? On the contrary.

Though a great ocean fishery was just a cast away and he was inundated with requests to be taken deep-sea fishing, Shula was like a marlin turning up its nose at a live mackerel. He would have no part of it.

"I told them, 'No thanks, I've been seasick a lot and I've seen all the fish I want to see.'

"So I turned to golf."

CHEECH MARIN

Cheech Marin was never a starving actor. Not when he had a fishing rod. Marin used to catch his dinner in front of his home on the beach in Malibu, California when he first moved there in the early 1970s.

"That's how I used to eat every day," he says. "I went fishing every day."

From the kelp beds, he caught rockfish, sculpin and calico bass, some as big as 10 pounds. He used a hand line, learning the method from neighbor Richard Ellis.

But meals weren't the only reason for rowing out onto the ocean. Marin found it peaceful, except for the few times a visitor would drop by unexpectedly.

"One time Richard and I were out there relaxing and heard this bang, like a shotgun," Marin recalls. "We didn't know what it was. I said, 'You hear that?' 'Yeah, I heard that. Where did it go?'

"We looked up and about 10 feet away from us popped up this big whale with an eye as big around as a basketball. He looked at us, we looked at him, and he looked at us, and he went on his merry way."

Marin learned something from this close encounter, something more than how startling the noise from a whale's blowhole can be.

"I can tell you what a whale smells like up close."

Chapter Six

Reel Passion

They are a breed of fishermen who just can't get enough. The desire to fish is as constant as a heartbeat. The craving to wet a line burns in their gut where the pilot light never goes out.

These are anglers who can spend hours on the water without catching a fish yet refuse to go home. "Just one more cast" turns into two, four, eight, 10 more casts.

These anglers plan their next fishing trip even before they get home from the last one. They are anglers who are in tune with nature, appreciate the scenery and serenity, and, most of all, relish the tug at the end of the line.

For whatever reason, this breed of angler is as enamored about fishing as parents are about their children.

The late Bing Crosby was such an angler. He enjoyed the pursuit of fish because it offered him anonymity. The fish failed to recognize the celebrity who was casting an artificial fly in its direction. To the fish, Crosby was just another angler.

"I'll tell you why I love fishing," Crosby once told legendary sports broadcaster Curt Gowdy. "Those fish don't give a damn if I can sing or if I've got all this money and everything. They really humble me and I think it's great. And anything I can do to escape Hollywood, get out of there and relax, that's what I'm looking for."

The story is the same for most celebrities. Fishing is an escape into a world without bright lights, adoring fans and the ever-present media.

As golf great Tiger Woods has often said when asked why he enjoys fishing so much, "Fish don't ask for autographs."

Friend and fellow golf professional Mark O'Meara introduced Woods to a rod and reel in 1997, showing his young prodigy there is more to life than just birdies and eagles.

Once he tried fly fishing, Woods was hooked. Alaska and Ireland became his favorite fly-fishing destinations. He often spends time fly fishing in Ireland on the way to or from the British Open.

While Woods remains serious about his golf, a passion for fishing began to burn in his soul, bringing him newfound happiness from the balance it helped produce in his life.

Before the 2001 PGA Championship, Woods talked with reporters about the hobby that allows him to escape.

"When you are out there, you're just away from a lot of different things, and your mind is free to just basically not think about anything," he said. "It's nice to have that atmosphere, to be able to have those kinds of outlets in your life. It's neat to be able to get away from things for a little bit."

Two legends from another era, long before Woods, often transformed their love of fishing into words. Legendary authors Ernest Hemingway and Zane Grey worked a rod and reel as adeptly as a typewriter.

Hemingway found fishing as a youth in the lakes and streams of Michigan and eventually discovered saltwater angling in Key West, Florida, and later in Cuba.

More than 50 years ago, Hemingway wrote *The Old Man and the Sea*, a masterpiece that earned him the Pulitzer Prize for fiction and the

Nobel Prize for literature. The tale is about an old fisherman making the catch of a lifetime in an unforgettable battle of dogged determination followed by utter disappointment.

Grey is best known for his western novels. His best-selling book *Riders of the Purple Sage* in 1910 brought him fame and fortune, enabling him to travel the world in search of battling fish.

He was known as a fishing trailblazer in Mexico, Central and South America, New Zealand, Australia and the South Pacific. The International Game Fish Association, the keeper of fishing world records, recognized Grey as a pioneering angler and great innovator. He held more than a dozen saltwater fishing world records in his day. It is difficult to imagine anybody more in tune with fishing than Grey.

"He fished everywhere—anywhere that he heard was exciting," says Michael Farrior, historian for the famed Avalon Tuna Club of Santa Catalina Island off Southern California. Grey, incidentally, was once a member of this historic club.

"Fishing was more than a sport to him," Farrior continues. "He was literally about proving his worth in life. I haven't ever read that, but I can assure you that's the case. The things he did, the lengths he went to. He wanted to get the first grander (a 1,000-pound fish), he wanted to hold world records all over and do a number of things. He was absolutely driven.

"I don't think there could be anybody more passionate about fishing. He seems to never have lost that child-like enthusiasm."

Besides Grey, numerous other celebrities escaped to Catalina Island to fish.

Silent-film star Charlie Chaplin, filmmaker Cecil B. DeMille and General George Patton, in his early days, made the fishing waters off Catalina their second home. Patton, whose family lived on the island, was known for his light-tackle prowess. He was a lieutenant when he eventually left the island to fight bigger battles elsewhere.

Winston Churchill loved fishing, too. He read about the Avalon Tuna Club in the international press. The stories about the phenomenal fishing at Catalina Island whetted his appetite for wetting a line in her waters. When the opportunity presented itself, Churchill traveled to the club in 1929. The visit is legendary.

A local angler took Churchill fishing. They weren't far from the clubhouse when Churchill hooked into, fought and landed a 125-pound

Silent-film star Charlie Chaplin proudly stands by the 162-pound
striped marlin he landed in 22 minutes off Catalina Island.
Photo courtesy of Michael Farrior/Tuna Club of Santa Catalina Island

Famous filmmaker Cecil B. DeMille took one hour and 18 minutes to boat this striped marlin off Catalina Island on September 18, 1919.
Photo courtesy of Michael Farrior/Tuna Club of Santa Catalina Island

Winston Churchill poses with the 125-pound striped marlin he caught at Catalina Island. He had heard how epic the big-game fishing was for members of the Tuna Club. His visit to the club in 1929 was short, however. It took him only 15 minutes to land the fish and his outing was all of 90 minutes.
Photo courtesy of Michael Farrior/Tuna Club of Santa Catalina Island

marlin. It took him all of 15 minutes to land the fish. From the time he left the clubhouse, caught the fish and returned, only 90 minutes elapsed. He made it look easy, Farrior said.

"I can sure see why you chaps enjoy it here," Churchill said as he savored a cigar and a scotch at the clubhouse afterward. "It's got everything you'd want. Great fishing, great camaraderie. This is a lot of fun."

Soon after, he put out his cigar, drained his drink and was gone.

"He left as fast as he came," Farrior says.

The fact Churchill was able to spend only a little time at Catalina but still made the 26-mile crossing from Los Angeles is testament to the enjoyment he received from fishing.

On those same waters, a love affair with the ocean and the fish in it blossomed inside the heart of a man who was no less passionate than Grey, Hemingway, Woods, Churchill or Crosby.

The late Milton Shedd epitomized the fisherman who couldn't get enough, who wanted to make just one more cast, who couldn't wait to plan his next fishing trip.

It started with the curiosity of a four-year-old.

As a youngster, Shedd walked onto the Santa Monica Pier, peered into the water and became mesmerized by a school of smelt. He wanted to learn everything he could about smelt. What they ate, what ate them, where they went at night, why they hung out under a pier.

This simple walk onto the pier began a lifetime of examining the ocean and its underwater world so full of life. Shedd co-founded Sea World, founded the Hubbs-Sea World Research Institute and helped create the UCLA Marine Science Center.

He was a pioneer in marine conservation and one heck of a fisherman.

The best example of his fascination for fish came when he was a commercial swordfish fisherman. Shedd and his partner, Tim Hauser, anchored their boat for the night off San Clemente Island, off the Southern California coast. When Hauser awoke at three in the morning to relieve himself, he was startled at what he saw under the lights shining into the water from the stern. A hand grasping the rail. Suddenly, it disappeared and he could hear a splash. Then the hand reappeared on the rail. It disappeared again with a splash.

"His first thought was that dad had fallen overboard," recalls Bill Shedd, Milton's son. "But he soon realized he was OK. He walked to the back of the boat and stood where dad couldn't see him. Dad was on his hands and knees on the swim step, reaching out as far as he could to try to catch some baitfish in his hand. Then he would look at them like, 'Hey, I want to know what you're all about.' Then he'd let it go and he'd reach way out again and grab another one. He'd put his hand on the rail to pull himself back up."

Shedd was a quiet sort. Bragging about a catch wasn't his nature, and heaven knows he had plenty to boast about. He was more behind the scenes, low-key.

His love for fishing is perhaps best depicted in the last year of his life when he was determined to continue fishing despite the debilitating bone cancer that wracked his body.

Eight months before his death, he told his doctor he wanted to go fishing. Walking was difficult for Shedd, who limped badly as the bone cancer ate away at his hip. The doctor couldn't imagine him on the swaying deck of a fishing boat, so he said no. Shedd couldn't imagine not going.

"Well, I'm going fishing," he said.

And so he did. Shedd, his son and a group of friends went on a multi-day trip aboard the Polaris Supreme from San Diego. They caught albacore tuna at Guadalupe Island off Baja California and were having a great time.

After a few days, the seas started getting rough under 30-knot winds. The forecast called for more wind the next day, prompting the skipper to gather everyone around and ask them if they were ready to go home. A few had already agreed they would vote to start for home. Not Shedd.

"Dad shot his hand up in the air and said, 'Man, there's fish to be caught, let's stay here and fish. I'm for fishing,'" Bill Shedd recalls.

"Everybody else kind of looked around. We all wanted to go home because we were just getting beat on. The other guys didn't know that dad had cancer. They just knew he was 78 years old and was limping a little bit. They just thought, 'Geez, if he's voting to stay then I sure can't vote to go home.'"

The vote was unanimous. They stayed.

On an ocean resembling water churning inside a washing machine, they fished another day and caught several more albacore and Milton Shedd landed more than his share.

Two months before his death, Shedd, his son Bill and Greg Stotesbury went halibut fishing on Stotesbury's boat. Shedd was in a wheelchair by then. It was tied down to keep him in place. Shedd couldn't bait his hook or cast, but he could set the hook and reel in fish. He out-fished his son again.

When Stotesbury asked Milt if he was ready to go in, he didn't respond.

"He just didn't have it in him to say, 'Yeah, I think we should quit fishing,'" Bill Shedd says. "Never in my life do I remember him ever saying, 'Let's stop fishing.' He just would never want to stop.

"So I said, 'Well, yeah Greg, I think it's time to go in.' Dad looked up at me and said, 'Bill, do we have to go in now?' I said, 'Yeah, it's time.' Dad says, 'Well, if everybody else wants to go in then I guess we'd better go in.' He just didn't have it in him to be the guy to say let's stop."

Three days before his death, Shedd was extremely ill and couldn't speak but indicated his desire to go fishing. He could still turn the reel handle and work a fish.

They took him to a local country club to fish for bass from one of its ponds. A hook was baited and tossed out for him. He took the rod. Eight-inch largemouth bass would take the bait and Shedd set the hook. A fish that could be brought in within seconds was played for several minutes at a time.

Bill Shedd was puzzled. Why was it taking his father so long to bring the fish in? After watching him catch two or three fish this way, it finally dawned on him.

"He would lift the rod up and then the fish would run back down into the weeds, so he could feel it pull," Bill Shedd explains. "Then he'd just sit there with it and just feel the fish on the other end."

"Hey, dad," Bill said to his father. "You're enjoying the feeling of the fish pulling at the end of the line, aren't you?"

Shedd hadn't spoken in days and had worn a permanent frown on his face as a result of his painful condition.

The elder Shedd looked at his son, pulled the fish up and pointed to the end of the twitching rod. Suddenly, like the sun's rays piercing through an opening in the clouds, the scowl on Shedd's face melted into a radiant, affirmative smile.

Milton Shedd lived to feel that tug of the line. He possessed the passion of which we speak. The late baseball great Ted Williams had it. Golfer Greg Norman has it and so does actor Kevin Costner.

"I feel badly for somebody who says, 'I just don't get what fishing is about,'" Costner says. "I guess you've had to grow up with it or something."

Who knows exactly when this fishing seed is planted? Whenever it is, it seems to take hold of fishermen like a barbed hook and doesn't let go.

Just one more cast...

TED WILLIAMS

Everybody knows a baseball bat was like a magic wand in the hands of Ted Williams. Yet the human hitting machine was much more impressed with the catches he made over the years.

They were countless, momentous and memorable, and certainly deserving of enshrinement into the Hall of Fame.

The *Fishing* Hall of Fame.

Williams was hailed as the purest hitter in baseball history and his immortality in the sport is assured. If it had been up to him, however, people would remember him most for his fishing.

"I belong at least in one (Hall of Fame), and that's fishing," Williams said in a 1998 phone interview.

Surely Williams is the only person who felt that what he did with a rod and reel overshadowed what he did with a baseball bat. He honestly believed he was better at fishing than at baseball.

"I want to tell you something and this will sum it up for you," he explained. "If I had my life to live over again and I could take fishing or baseball, I'd take fishing and I'll tell you why: I don't think I would do as well in baseball if I had to do it over again. I know I'd have done as good in fishing.

"Fishing to me has been such an important part of my life—the tranquillity, the beauty and the expectations of so many things. I look back and think, I had as much fun tying flies as I did fishing. I had as much fun rigging up rods and reels and balancing them out. I had as much fun BS-ing on the side as you ever saw. The real joys are fishing on a beautiful stream and tying your own flies.

"I'll tell you, wading on a bonefish flat when there's a few fish tailing and you know there's some big ones is just as big a thrill as you can get because you have to make the perfect cast, you can't disturb things

Ted Williams, a prolific and avid angler, talks during the ceremony
of his induction into the IGFA Fishing Hall of Fame in 2000.
Curt Gowdy, left, called him the best all-around fisherman he ever knew.
Photo courtesy of the IGFA

too much and you have to have an expertise to hook them and play them on a fly rod. Nothing could beat that for me."

Not even a home run.

Baseball honored Williams by inducting him into the Hall of Fame in 1966. The National Fresh Water Fishing Hall of Fame enshrined him in 1995.

In 2000, his longtime friend and fishing partner Curt Gowdy helped induct Williams into the Fishing Hall of Fame of the International Game Fish Association, fishing's equivalent to Cooperstown.

Williams, helped to the stage from his wheelchair, accepted the honor with pride and exhilaration.

"He was really thrilled," Gowdy said. "It was funny. All the honors he had and everything, you thought this was the greatest honor he ever had in his life."

Maybe it was.

Ted Williams caught the fishing bug from a neighbor in his hometown of San Diego when he turned 13 or thereabouts. The neighbor showed him some largemouth bass he'd caught and the bait-casting outfit he used. Williams was wide-eyed.

"I was just carried away with the whole damn thing," he said. "Then, by God, he took me fishing. From there on, I started to fish."

Living in San Diego was a fishing boon to Williams. At his doorstep was the Pacific Ocean and a prolific fishery. He caught yellowtail, albacore and barracuda.

One day during the Great Depression in the early 1930s, Williams was on a boat that landed 98 barracuda. Most of the catch was given away to many grateful people at the dock.

"We wrapped them up in paper and gave them to everybody," Williams recalled. "You know, everybody's having a tough time then."

As his baseball career blossomed, so did his fly-fishing skills. Before every spring training with the Boston Red Sox, Williams fished the Florida Keys, where he discovered fishing with a fly.

One day, as he fished with a plug in vain, Williams eyed a gentleman catching fish after fish using a fly-fishing outfit.

"The guy on the bank has a big snook on with a fly rod and I thought, 'Geez Louise!'" Williams recalled. "I stopped and I went down and I talked to him."

The man caught a 12-pound snook. The fact he was catching them left and right on flies excited Williams.

"That thoroughly convinced me that was the way to go. Then, the next year I went down there with a fly rod and I murdered them. Oh, boy!"

Williams, the expert fly fisherman, was born.

Ever the perfectionist, Williams became as proficient in fly fishing as a fishing guide and eventually wrote a book, *Fishing for the Big Three*, about his three favorite fly-fishing targets: Tarpon, bonefish and Atlantic salmon.

He caught tarpon and bonefish in the Florida Keys and Atlantic salmon in the Miramichi River in New Brunswick, Canada, where he owned a fishing camp.

Gowdy once wrote that "before Ted was done, he'd caught and recorded 1,000 tarpon caught on the fly. He also caught 1,000 bonefish and 1,000 Atlantic salmon on a fly. Now that's a triple crown to brag about."

Not only did Williams use flies, but he tied them.

"He was a very good fly tier," Gowdy said. "That's how he spent his time on the road, tying flies up in his room. He didn't want to go out. People would mob him. That was his hobby, tying these flies."

Gowdy fished with Williams more than a hundred times and called him the best all-around fisherman he ever knew.

"Fishing was good for him," Gowdy said. "It got him away from the pressures he had. He got a lot of relaxation and enjoyment from it."

And, heaven knows, a surplus of memorable moments.

There was the 1,234-pound black marlin Williams caught off Casa Blanca, Peru, and the 500-pound thresher shark he landed in New Zealand, and the permit he bet Gowdy he'd catch during the filming of an episode of *American Sportsman.*

Production of the outdoors TV show wasn't going well. After two days, neither Williams nor Gowdy had caught a permit. They were getting ready to scrub the show when Williams bet Gowdy $500 he'd catch one the next day. Gowdy refused to bet.

After failing to catch one in the morning, Williams bet Gowdy $1,000 he'd catch one that afternoon. This time, Gowdy took the bet and true to form, Williams came through in the clutch. He landed a 20-pound permit and saved the show. They then caught several more.

Boston Red Sox legend Ted Williams often fished the Florida Keys before spring training. He caught this bonefish during a fishing trip to Florida in February 1955.
AP/WWP

"I think I caught six and he caught two," Williams recalled. "The funny part of it is, that when this was shown on national TV, he caught six and I got two. I've always kidded him about that."

Williams loved to needle others, and at times he could be as abrasive as shark skin. But the guard came down when talking about fishing. The spark in his voice was undeniable.

"You know, I haven't been very well the last five years, and I want to tell you something," said Williams, debilitated by strokes in the later stages of his life. "I lay in bed and I think. I think about baseball. Then I start thinking about fishing and the different experiences and the different fish and the different people I've met and the different flies I've tied, and how I loved to rig up tackle, and always when I rigged them up nothing was better. I can't do it any more. I can't see well enough."

But the wonderful daydreams about fishing he recollected with 20/20 clarity.

The most poignant story Williams told was the time in 1993 when he was fly fishing the Miramichi River and hooked into a fish of a lifetime, an Atlantic salmon.

The day was windy, rainy and cold. Only a passionate angler would attempt to fish in such conditions.

"I'm starting to wade down the pool and I'm telling you, I'll never forget this in my life: The most beautiful salmon. He jumped, oh, about 30, 40 feet from me, straight up. I saw the whole fish. I saw everything. I've never seen anything as pretty as that and I've never in the world had ever hung one like that.'"

With a steady rain misting his glasses, the cold digging into his bones and the fish not cooperating, Williams decided to retreat to the cabin, warm up and change into dry clothes.

After lunch, he went back down to the pool where he'd seen the big fish and started casting again.

"Ahhh! There he is!" Williams recalled. "I got him on! I realized it was a good fish."

Roy Curtis, his longtime friend and guide, watched the proceedings from a bluff overhead. Old and ill, Curtis slowly shuffled down the hill to help Williams land the fish.

"I'll never forget the picture looking back up on the cottage, and I knew he wasn't feeling very well," Williams said. "He was getting into his waders as fast as he could to come down and help me."

They netted the fish, estimated its length at 43 inches and let it go. Later, in the warmth of the cottage, the fish story was completed.

"I said, 'Roy, I think that fish weighed 31, 32 pounds.' He's caught hundreds and hundreds and hundreds of salmon, though he never ever caught one that big, and he always said, 'Ted, if you don't call him 35 pounds, you're cheating yourself.' That's the line he used. 'If you don't call him 35 pounds, you're cheating yourself.' So I've always called it 35 pounds.

"Anyway, that's the story.

"It was one of my greatest thrills because that fish jumped up 30 feet ahead of me as I was in the pool. He jumped up to show me he was there, you know? I'll never forget how impressed I was with that fish coming out of the water. And, by God, I caught him right down in the same area with the smallest single fly I've ever caught a big fish on: A little single 8. It was a little green buck fly, which they called a conrad. It is as good a fly as you could throw in the Miramichi."

As memorable as this catch was, the fact Curtis was there to help made it all the more treasured to Williams. It was the last fish Curtis saw Williams land.

"Roy was dying," Williams said. "He had a liver-kidney problem. He died that winter. He was a great guy, and I'll never forget him. He was one of the many, many, many memories I've had about fishing."

"I've had so much fun fishing." —Ted Williams, 1918-2002

KEVIN COSTNER

With arms and legs, Kevin Costner clung upside from a log over a pool of water, fully aware of his fate. He was going to get wet. It was just a matter of time before gravity delivered him with a splash, like a drop from a leaky faucet.

The object of this misadventure was a trout, a rather large trout Kevin failed to catch with hook and line from the stream. Frustrated but determined, he went home and fetched his father's fishing net.

He was seven years old.

With net in hand and unsuspecting prey swimming below, Kevin inched along atop the log, straddling it with his legs as if riding a pony. His intention was to net the fish that had turned its nose at his bait.

"Somehow in reaching, I lost my balance and I slid underneath the log," Costner explains. "The water is flowing five inches from my back, I have the net and, for the first time in my life, I suddenly realized I've done something really stupid.

"So I hung there with all my strength, going, 'Well, I'm not getting wet until I'm really tired.' I had three or four minutes of true thinking about how foolish I was that there's nobody around and that I could've been in real danger. I thought about risks outweighing wanting to get something. I actually had these intellectual thoughts at seven."

Alas, magic would not be pulled out of his thinking cap. The helping hand he so desperately needed to escape this predicament was not forthcoming. There was—dare we say?—no way out.

"I fell straight in," Costner says.

Soaked, Kevin stubbornly waded the pool of that stream near his childhood home in Ojai, California and finally netted the fish. He felt pathetic.

"I rode home on my bicycle wet and in my net I had this goofy-looking trout with bulging eyes and clearly not edible," he remembers. "When I got home, my dad said, 'Awww, get that thing out of here, you can't eat that fish!'"

So Kevin discarded the fish and digested a serving of humility.

The story is as much symbolic as humorous. Going out on a limb is typical Kevin Costner. Risk-taking, whether in business, acting or even fishing, is part of his makeup. It is among the many traits that were woven into the fabric of his character at an early age.

A love for fishing, nature and the outdoors also took root in Costner in his childhood home of Ojai, where he ventured into the country day and night by himself, guided by the spirit of adventure.

As a kid, he extracted venom from a live rattlesnake after getting the impression from a TV show that he could get money for it.

He once built an Everglades-type boat. To line the cracks, he chewed 100 pieces of bubble gum and ate Fritos with each piece to make a concoction similar to adobe. It worked. "It didn't leak," he says.

As a teenager, he and a friend got into a canoe Kevin built and rode it 400 yards down a hillside of weeds and into Irvine Lake, a pay-to-fish lake in Orange County, California. They couldn't afford the entry fee.

As an adult, Costner enjoys not only recreational fishing but free-dive spearfishing. It's a risk-taking sport in which you hold your breath,

Kevin Costner enjoys free diving and spearfishing. This 58-pound halibut he speared near Santa Cruz Island off Southern California was close to a state record. Diving partner Billy Kendig holds the monster fish.
Photo courtesy of Kevin Costner

swim down some 30 feet and hunt for fish. In July 2000, he speared a 58-pound halibut off Santa Cruz Island in Southern California. The fish was so strong, it was speared a second time, and Costner got help from a friend to pull it up.

"That is interesting to me, the stalk," he explains. "The free diving is interesting, too, because you have to have your wits about you. If you actually tie into a pretty big fish, what happens is your instincts of not wanting to let go takes over and maybe you go a little deeper than you're supposed to and you make a mistake. You can kill yourself.

"There has to be a moment in time where you give yourself that 10 seconds to get to the top. It's interesting. It totally feeds me."

Living on the edge, that's Kevin.

This daring demeanor and nose for adventure are perhaps best evidenced in the summer of 1975 when he decided to work as a commercial fisherman on the northern coast of California. It was an odd choice, given his propensity for becoming seasick.

"I don't know what I was thinking about wanting to go commercial fishing," he says. "I had only been on a sportfishing boat two times and I got sick both times, really violently sick."

Nevertheless, the spirit of adventure led him to Eureka, California, in search of a boat to work on. If he couldn't find a fishing job, Costner planned to work as a logger, though this was his least favorite option, adventuresome or not.

Luckily, after three days, Kevin found work on a salmon boat and willed himself not to get ill. It worked. He didn't get sick once.

For three months, Costner toiled on the decks of 40-foot commercial fishing boats. It was hard work. Six lines went straight down into the water. A dozen leaders with hooks were attached to each line. The leader was 80-pound test. Kevin would bring them up by hand and gaff the salmon that were legal size. Undersized fish were released. The bigger ones were shot to ensure they wouldn't wiggle free.

One time, Costner discovered a six-foot shark at the end of the line. Not wanting to lose the 80-pound leader, Kevin wrapped the line around his hand as the fish came to the surface in a death spiral. Inexplicably, the skipper shot the shark.

Big mistake.

"It woke him up and he just went ballistic," Kevin explains. "It took off. The line ripped through the skin of my hand. There was a moment where it was flesh tone. Then all of a sudden—shoooo—it went to blood. It spun the line out off my hand. That was a shock."

A scar on his hand serves as a reminder of the experience.

A bigger scare was the time he and his captain were caught in "Perfect Storm" conditions. The boat climbed up 50-foot walls of water and dropped down the other side. Waves lapped over the bow. For 24 hours it was tense times—high adventure on the high seas.

It was an unforgettable summer.

"I loved it out there."

Costner enjoys fishing with rod and reel for the adventure, for the time spent with nature, for the solitude. It's for the fish, too, but catching fish is the proverbial icing in the creel.

What if he doesn't catch anything?

"I feel a measure of disappointment, but I don't ever feel like I'll never go back," he says. "Other people, it's like, 'I won't ever go back.' All it does for me is it increases my desire to go back."

Go back enough times and sooner or later the fish of a lifetime will be at the end of the line.

Costner's "fish of a lifetime" was hooked one summer while on a two-week cruise through the Inside Passage of Alaska on a rented yacht with his then-wife Cindy and kids.

The 60-foot vessel was anchored inside a cove. It was early morning. Kevin was at the stern jigging for rock cod. The skipper was getting ready to raise the anchor when the unexpected occurred.

"I felt something really hit hard," Kevin says. "Then all of a sudden, there was just slack. I realized that it was swimming up and away and creating the slack. So I quickly reeled and brought the tension to bare. I knew I had something big. I kept fighting it."

The skipper didn't appreciate the gravity of the situation as he kept pulling up the anchor. Costner yelled for him to stop and continued playing the fish for 10 minutes.

"Finally it came up and I saw a flash and it was huge," Kevin says. "It looked to me to be 40, 50 pounds. I couldn't believe it. I'd never landed a fish like that."

Now the skipper was interested. He quickly went for the net. Ah, yes, the net. Costner had noticed it earlier on the trip. He told the skipper they should get a bigger one just in case. They never did.

*Anne and Lily, Kevin Costner's daughters,
pose with their Alaskan catch of the day.*
Photo courtesy of Kevin Costner

"The net wasn't big enough, and I could see that it wasn't big enough," Kevin says. "I said, 'No, no, don't, it's not big enough. Wait, I want to tire him out a little bit more.'"

The net might work if the fish was played to exhaustion, or so Kevin thought. With a lively fish, chances were slim. The skipper didn't comprehend.

"He didn't know anything about fishing and he just got really excited and I was saying, 'No, don't, not yet.' He just went down after it with me saying, 'No, don't,' and he knocked it off the hook.

"I was stunned. I had to kind of gather myself because I had fished all my life to catch a fish like that. I've fished in every mud hole that I saw along the way since I was little. So something like that was really a trophy.

"What was great was the fish was giving me problems. I was out-gunned. I had no business catching that fish and it proved it. Had I had the right net, though, I would've caught it. It was one of those dumb-luck things that I'd seen throughout my life, like the little kid catching the biggest trout of the day. I never had that kind of luck. And there it was.

"I wasn't with a guide, it was just me dinking around and finding it—on a rock cod rig! You can't fault him for having desire to net it. Anyway, he's a captain, he ain't no fisherman. I was disappointed. I remember probably laying down with Cindy that night, being kind of a child going, 'Should've caught that fish, that son of a...'"

Eventually, Kevin would land a 40-pound salmon, the treasured catch of a lifetime.

Yet when it comes to fishing treasures, Costner's most precious jewel didn't come with a rod and reel in his hands but in those of children catching much smaller fish from a lake on his property in Aspen, Colorado.

"That is probably the best fishing story I have," he says.

The home Kevin bought in Aspen is one he imagined as a kid. Lake. Stream. Wild trout. Wildlife bounding about. A cabin in the wilderness. Nature—35 acres of it.

"It's heaven," he says.

Especially for kids going through hell.

A few miles away, former tennis star Andrea Jaeger runs the Kids' Stuff Foundation, a camp for terminally ill children. She once took a group fishing to a lake that was over an hour away. The kids didn't catch a thing.

When Kevin heard this, he called Jaeger and offered the use of his lake. He purchased and planted 300 rainbow trout, since the wild brook trout in the lake are weary and difficult to catch.

The kids had a blast.

"I looked out on my lake and there were 20 kids that were bald," Kevin says. "They had lost all their hair. I had paid a lot of money for this land, a lot more than I thought I should, more money than I ever dreamed possible. And I looked out and saw them fishing. They had these great big bobbers going straight down. Some kids were launching fish onto shore, like tuna. Others just couldn't believe it.

A proud father-son, Kodak fishing moment as Kevin Costner
holds the German brown his son, Joe, caught in Aspen.
Photo courtesy of Kevin Costner

"I had imagined this home since I was seven years old and I realized I wasn't even the person getting the joy out of fishing, they were. Yet I was getting a lot of joy watching them. I thought, 'You know what? No matter what I paid for that property, it was worth it that day.' It really was, and they continue to come."

They come on one condition, presumably. That they stay away from any overhanging logs in the nearby stream. Oh yes, the property has logs.

"There are always logs when there are streams and there is always slipping," Kevin says, philosophically. "I guess when you don't slip anymore, it means you're probably not trying to cross anything. It means you're probably not trying to get anywhere.

"If you're going to go somewhere, you're maybe going to slip. You've got to take the chance of getting wet. I think that's what fishing is about more than anything else...

"Maybe that's why I climbed that log."

GREG NORMAN

Everything ached. Hands, arms, shoulders, legs—the entire body. As the sun melted into the horizon, cold and exhaustion gripped Greg Norman while he endured the fight of his life.

Clad in t-shirt and shorts, Norman was playing tug-o-war with a potential world-record Great White Shark, estimated at 1,900 pounds.

Norman, a professional golfer known as The Great White Shark, was using 50-pound-test line and fishing with stand-up gear. Most big-game anglers fish from a fighting chair. Norman wasn't taking this fish sitting down.

Three times Norman got the fish to the boat only to see it take another run. The fourth time was the charm. The Great White Shark was victorious.

If you go deep-sea fishing with Greg Norman, you better have taken your seasickness pills because he isn't turning back should you turn the matching hue of a putting green.

"I stipulate before I take anybody if you get sick, you're not coming in," Norman said. "That's your choice."

Norman is serious. It's happened before.

"I won't go in, especially if the fishing is good," he said.

Norman takes his friends fishing on occasion, yet he prefers to pursue his favorite hobby on his own. That's part of the allure to fishing.

"To me, it's the solitude," he said. "I like to fish on my own because I like the challenge. I can sit there in my cockpit for hours on end and not get a bite and it seems like it's gone in five minutes.

"I like watching the bait. I like the surprise element of what's going to happen. I was fishing where you go four or five days without even seeing a fish then, boom, here comes that 800-pounder right out of the blue. She comes sailing down with a couple of males beside her. Then you try to bait the fish, get a doubleheader on black marlin and all of a sudden the excitement is there. So I'm pretty much a solitude fisherman."

And a pretty good one at that.

"I grew up on the Great Barrier Reef," he said. "If you didn't know how to fish there, you didn't know how to fish."

Norman knows fishing. He has fished for steelhead, cutthroat trout and largemouth bass, but saltwater not freshwater is his passion. Billfish, any kind of billfish, is his preference.

"To me, the biggest thrill is trying to bait a big fish," he explained.

He will never forget the day in Mexico he caught and released 28 sailfish out of 43 bites. He had triple hookups and fought them one at a time, keeping the other rods in their holders.

"Over 50 percent on sailfish is pretty good when you've got that many going, especially triple-headers, being as you can cut them off and they all go in a different direction. We had controlled mayhem there for a few moments.

"My boat captain said, 'Look, you may never see this again. Let's enjoy it for what it is.' It wasn't like we were the only boat. There were others, but we had the most. We were the most successful."

Another time, he caught and released 23 bonefish in Belize.

Norman has caught black marlin, white marlin, blue marlin, swordfish—just about any kind of ocean fish with the exception of bluefin tuna and a spearfish, though he's probably caught those by now, too.

But the most memorable fish was that 1,900-pound Great White Shark he hooked in the late 1980s.

"That to me, was probably my best fishing moment," Norman said.

Norman's nickname was derived from an offhand comment he made during the 1981 Masters about how he hated sharks and would love to shoot them. He changed his tune when he came face to face with Great White Sharks for four days while scuba diving in shark cages in the waters off Adelaide, Australia.

The only shooting that was done was with cameras. Footage was taken of sharks eating out of Norman's hand. His hatred for this massive creature of the sea dissolved into fascination.

One day, the captain of his diving boat asked Norman, "Have you ever thought about trying to get a world-record great white on 50-pound test?"

Norman gave it a thought. Usually when he goes fishing he takes his own standup tackle that fits him like an old shoe, one with properly fitting back and leg braces. He didn't have anything on this trip.

"What have you got?" Norman asked.

"Well, I've got this 50-pound straight-butt rod," the captain replied.

"How am I going to get any leverage with a straight butt?" said Norman, who uses a curved-butted rod that allows for better leverage. "Oh, what the hell, I might as well try."

So Norman and Gary Stuve, a charter-boat captain who often skippered Norman's fishing trips, went with the dive-boat captain in quest of a world record. Stuve was the first mate and gaffer.

The hookup came in the afternoon and soon it became evident neither the tackle nor the captain were adequate.

Norman jerry-rigged a shoulder harness with his belt because his hands were getting so tired and he couldn't grasp the rod any longer.

The boat captain, a shark expert without much fishing expertise, wasn't competent enough to back the boat down on the fish. There was nothing Norman could do about the tackle, but he could do something about the captain.

"I said, 'Gary, you get up there and just take the helm. You know how I fish, I know how you run the boat, this is the only way we're going to catch this fish.' The owner of the boat was pretty good. He let him take over. That's when we had a bit more of a chance to do it."

It was a classic battle: The Great White Shark vs. The Great White Shark.

Not many words were spoken. Norman was in quiet concentration for more than four hours in a classic game of give and take. Pull up, reel down. Pull up, reel down. The battle between shark and man was wearing on Norman. The pain was beginning to take its toll when finally, Norman got the fish up near the boat for the fourth time.

The end was near. Then it happened. The knot broke at the swivel on the leader. The fish was lost.

After four hours, 43 minutes, the fight was over. Yet Norman wasn't devastated. He was relieved.

"We lost her at the boat, thank God," he explained. "I was happy for her to swim away.

"I'm glad she's still out there somewhere. She deserves to be alive. I had a great fight. I'm not a killer. I tag every fish I catch. Most of the time, if I'm out fishing, I'll say to the captain, 'If you think this is the fish of the year or a record, maybe I'll keep it, but tell me during the fight and then I'll decide.' I've never mounted a sailfish or marlin or sword-fish. I just tag and release."

This fish was different. This might have been one for the record books in the day Great White Sharks were legal to catch. Norman claimed the estimated 1,900-pound great white would have beaten the existing line-class record by 400 or 500 pounds, though the record for 50 pound is 1,876 pounds.

The exact weight will remain a mystery. What is certain is that it defeated The Shark.

When the battle ended, Norman went inside the boat's cabin and laid down. He was cold and spent, not an ounce of energy remaining.

"You get in a little bit of shock, I suppose is what it is," he said. "You're physically tired and mentally tired. That was it. I couldn't even drink a beer. I felt sick because of the fatigue of it all."

To Norman, this was his personal version of *The Old Man and the Sea* by Ernest Hemingway. It was a classic tale, one Norman will forever cherish.

"It was one of the most memorable experiences I've ever had off the golf course."

Chapter Seven

When the Shark Bites

The movie *Jaws* struck fear into anybody who ever dipped a toe into saltwater. Many vowed never to swim in the ocean again, believing to do so would mean possibly becoming dinner for a Great White Shark.

In 1975, Peter Benchley's best-selling book was turned into this priceless and timeless horror flick that scared the bejeebers out of moviegoers, and left swimmers and divers wondering if the water would ever be safe. The Steven Spielberg-directed blockbuster about an enormous great white preying on unsuspecting swimmers off Amity Island probably produced a nightmare for every dollar it made.

Unfortunately, *Jaws* did more than cause heart rates to flutter. The terrifying tale stole the heart and soul of this magnificent creature, tarnishing its reputation. Sharks are not the scary monsters Hollywood portrayed them to be. In fact, the great white is not a man-eater as many believe. Sure, it has and does attack humans but usually by mistake. A diver in a black wetsuit and fins swimming near the surface becomes a seal or sea lion in the eyes of a great white.

In his book *Shark Trouble* in 2002, Benchley writes about shark behavior, the odds of getting attacked and how to swim safely in the ocean. He basically debunks the possibility of a real-life man-hunting shark like the one he created. He says in the book and has said in subsequent interviews that he couldn't possibly write *Jaws* today, now that he better understands this massive beast.

"Even he recognizes the damage that that did to the resource," said Keith Poe, a noted shark expert in Southern California who has tagged thousands of sharks and preaches conservation religiously. "People used to have zero respect for them and they thought it was something we needed to rid the earth of. It's not nearly as bad as it used to be."

The importance of preserving sharks to keep the underwater ecosystem in balance is fortunately a message that is starting to spread among fishermen, many of whom have learned the precious tool of catch and release.

"I think that those who use the water frequently—surfers, divers and fishermen—best understand and respect the white shark," said Doug Obegi, formerly of the Ocean Conservancy. "In the same way that I don't want to be attacked by a grizzly bear but would be thrilled to see one in the wild—safely—so too are we torn about our relationship with the shark. Witness the rise in shark-cage diving around the world. We're becoming more curious and less afraid, I hope. I think the general public is starting to get it, too.

"Peter Benchley has been working with National Geographic for several years to try to dispel the fear that *Jaws* inspired, and to inspire people to come to understand and respect the white shark."

No question humans are fascinated by all kinds of sharks, though the great white, because of its enormous size and reputation, holds the greatest interest.

Many fishermen have encountered a Great White Shark while on the water. Some have watched it feed on a sea lion. Others have looked down to see one swim by, realizing their 18-foot boat was about the same length as the shark. Many have experienced a great white chomping down on their hooked tuna like it was an hors d'oeuvre on a toothpick.

Long-range anglers off Guadalupe Island in Baja, California, often are left with only the heads of 100-pound yellowfin tuna on their hooks.

Great whites frequent the waters off Southern California, too, but mako sharks and thresher sharks are the most common. Many believe the waters off the Los Angeles coast to be a nursery for mako sharks.

Further north, the Farrallon Islands off San Francisco is a famous breeding ground for seals and sea lions. It is an all-you-can-eat buffet for great whites. No question, they are present. However, despite the numbers of sharks, California has suffered only 11 fatal shark attacks out of 94 encounters since record-keeping began in the early 1950s, according to the California Department of Fish and Game.

If great whites were man-hunters, like in *Jaws*, they'd have all the surfers and divers and spearfishermen they could ever want off California. Yet statistics show people are much more likely to die being struck by lightning or a car than by getting attacked by a shark.

This is not to suggest the risk isn't there, just that the odds are nearly as long as a mule winning the Kentucky Derby. Stewart Graham is fully aware of those odds, which is why he approaches diving as if he's got an invisible shark shield around him. He believes he is shark-proof.

"My chances of being attacked are probably gone," the spearfisherman from Glendale, California says. "I'm probably the safest person to dive with."

That's because lightning doesn't usually strike twice. Graham is a rare breed, having come face to face with a shark set on doing a *Jaws* imitation.

"Be careful," Graham's wife Veronica told him on the eve of the San Diego Free Divers Bluewater Spearfishing meet in August 1999. "I've heard on the news there have been some shark sightings."

The next morning, sharks were the last thing on Graham's mind when he took a deep breath and descended with his speargun to 30 feet. He was searching for a yellowtail to shoot.

On top of the water in an 18-foot skiff were Danny Oliver of Solana Beach, California and Dave Oliver and his son, Kyle, of Huntington Beach, California. The spearfishing was slow, so none were eager to jump into the colder-than-usual water near the Coronado Islands south of San Diego.

Danny was just getting ready to jump in when Graham popped his head out of the water 50 yards away. He whistled and put his hand atop his head like a shark fin, as most people who saw *Jaws* did the next time they were in a pool.

"Danny, bring the boat around," Graham calmly called out. "There's a pretty good-sized shark over here."

Moments before, while searching for that elusive yellowtail, Graham spotted what looked to be a Great White Shark cruising right in front of him, 20 feet away, and it wasn't wearing a friendly expression.

Graham knew the look. He had encountered many sharks in 10 years of diving. He's been in the water with whitetip and blacktip sharks, reef sharks and hammerhead sharks in places such as the Galapagos Islands, Coco Island and Costa Rica. He recognized the sign language of an angry shark. With pectoral fins locked downward in attack mode, this shark seemed to be saying, *"Don't know what you're thinking, pal, but you're in my territory and I don't like it."*

Graham was content to get out of the water and avoid confrontation. Without commotion, he eased himself to the surface, trying to keep an eye on the shark's whereabouts as he ascended.

After alerting the others, Graham put his mask and snorkel back on and dropped three feet under the surface, searching.

From the corner of his eye, at four o'clock, he detected movement. He turned and looked. There was the shark, zeroing in on him like a torpedo. Graham needed to protect himself. He maneuvered around his five-and-a-half-foot Bluewater Hunter, a speargun designed to hunt big fish, and one that kicks like a mule.

"I remember turning that gun was an eternity," Graham recalls. "I had to turn the gun about 120 degrees."

Thoughts raced through his mind at warp speed. *If I poke at it, the shaft of the spear might come off and I will have played my only card wrong...if I use my knife; no, this thing is far too big for the knife. ... I'm just going to have to shoot it.*

The shark's mouth was wide open and charging, making erratic, side-to-side movements as it approached the human that infringed on its territory.

The shark was attacking.

"Not a doubt in my mind," Graham confirms.

For maximum impact, Graham needed to shoot when the shark was at least 12 feet away. Any closer and the six-foot spear would not have cleared the gun completely and would have been useless.

"So I said, 'I'm just going to wait until I get a decent shot and shoot,'" Graham remembers. "If he turns away, good, I may have enough time to get up into the boat. If not, I'm just going to shoot.'"

The point of no return arrived. The shark was not backing off. Mouth open. Head jerking side to side. It came straight at Graham. He aimed at the back of the shark's throat. He fired. At the same time, the shark's head jerked to the side.

"I knew I made contact, but I didn't know if I penetrated the fish enough to kill him," he says.

Graham wasn't about to stick around to find out. He released the float that connects to the line and spear, took two rapid kicks and was quickly into the safe confines of the boat.

The occupants of the boat were oblivious to the dangerous show playing out beneath them. Danny had thought Graham probably had seen a blue shark, a docile, harmless shark.

When he saw Graham hand his speargun to his brother Dave, Danny noticed the spear had been fired.

"Did you shoot him?" Danny asked.

"I had to, Danny, he was attacking me," Graham replied.

"Man, what you kill a shark for?" Danny chided.

He soon found out.

They motored over to pick up the float. Odd, it was sitting atop the water like a buoy. It didn't move. If big game was at the other end, it would be moving. Graham wondered if he had missed.

As he started pulling in the rope, Graham then felt the dead weight at the other end. Suddenly, Danny and the rest on board grasped the gravity of the situation, why Graham climbed out of the water with wide eyes, why Graham had to pull the trigger.

"It became very obvious as soon as we pulled it up and the jaws of that shark came out of the water head first," Danny says. "I just said, 'Holy shit! Stewart, I had no idea.'"

The massive jaws did not belong to a great white but to a mako shark—a nine-and-a-half-foot, 426-pound mako shark. This species seldom attacks humans but is considered dangerous. To an unsuspecting eye, it could be mistaken for a great white.

"I was sad because I killed the shark," says Graham, who understands the importance of shark conservation. "The last thing I wanted to do was kill the shark. I was very sorry I killed such a beautiful animal, but I was glad I had the right frame of mind to act the way I did, because I knew if I wouldn't have seen it before, I wouldn't be talking to you.

"This guy would've cut me in half. I would've been lunch for him."

They tied a rope around its tail and towed it back to San Diego where the shark was weighed and photographed. The spear was carved out of the body, the procedure serving as a sort of autopsy. The spear penetrated between the jaws and first gill, and straight into the spine. A one-in-a-million, debilitating shot. A life-saving shot.

Graham had been remarkably calm about the incident until that night when he returned home to his wife and two children. His knees buckled as reality sunk in. Had the shark sunk his teeth into him, had he not made the perfect shot, he might never have seen his wife and children again.

He cried.

For two months following the incident, Graham experienced nightmares about all the things that could've gone wrong: having the wrong gun, the spear bouncing off the shark, not seeing the shark first, being attacked from a blind spot. Once or twice a week, Graham awoke in a cold sweat.

A month later, he returned to ride the horse that bucked him off. He went diving again.

"I remember that very next dive, everything looked like a shark," he recalls. "Anything that moved. I was kind of paranoid."

Kelp, sea lions and even shadows looked like sharks, images Graham had to shake from his mind.

"After the first dive, I forgot about it," he says. "I said, 'I cannot be paranoid the rest of my life.'"

He dives with confidence now, knowing the odds, knowing his experience was an anomaly not likely to be repeated.

But he still thinks about it. In the corner of his mind are the jaws coming to eat him. That he will never forget. A reminder hangs in his living room. On the wall in a frame are those intimidating jaws.

"Not a day goes by..." Graham says, his thought trailing off. "I see those jaws there and I always thank the good Lord up there that He gave me a second chance."

KATHY IRELAND

The shark rose from the depths and headed straight for Kathy Ireland as she was scuba diving in 100 feet of water with friends who were spearfishing.

The super model tensed. For a change, she was behind the camera, taking photos using an underwater camera. But she wished something else were in her hands.

"I was thinking I wished I would've had a spear gun like everyone else," Ireland says.

Defenseless, Ireland aimed her camera at the shark and snapped off a picture, and the shark swam away.

"I was so nervous, the picture didn't really turn out that well," she says. "It was blurry and out of focus."

Of course, there was no need for alarm. This huge shark was hardly a man-eater. It was a whale shark, a harmless plankton feeder with small teeth.

Nevertheless, it was big enough to cause a scare—and a shaky shutterbug.

MICHAEL CHIKLIS

Three days before his wedding, actor Michael Chiklis went fishing for marlin, caught a huge shark instead and turned into a boiled lobster as a result.

The TV star of *The Shield* was as red as a well-done crustacean after suffering serious sunburn and sunstroke while catching a 330-pound hammerhead shark in June 1992.

"It took three hours to land," Chiklis explains. "When she hit, I wasn't expecting it. So I was bare-chested and hadn't put on the suntan cream yet. I had no hat on, so I got sunstroke terribly.

"The next day, my wife was balling her eyes out. She thought I wasn't paying attention to her. It's just that I couldn't keep my head up because I had boiled my brains. I had such terrible sunstroke that I was like, passing out. She was saying, 'You don't want to get married, you hate me.'"

The misunderstanding was soon resolved and the wedding went on as planned. Fortunately for Chiklis, the boiled lobster look dissolved before he said, "I do."

"By then, I was OK," he says. "My color had returned. I had a nice tan at that point, actually."

BILLY DEAN

Swimming with sharks in the Bahamas was not enough to prepare Billy Dean for a frightening encounter with another swimming creature in the lake he lives on outside of Nashville.

The country music star is a free-diving spearfisherman, capable of holding his breath and diving down 50 feet. One day he was spearfishing for non-gamefish catfish in Centerhill Lake.

At 20 feet deep, Dean couldn't see all that well. Visibility was only about five feet.

"I went to spear a big, old catfish and I found out it was about as long as I was," Dean recalls. "It was the biggest fish I'd seen in the lake. It scared me to death. Back to the top I went. I left my gear, everything. I thought I saw a shark in the lake."

Later, he cautiously swam back down and retrieved his equipment. Dean never saw the huge catfish again. He hopes he never does.

"He would've drowned me if I'd have shot him," Dean says. "He'd have drug me around. I would not have been able to make it."

MEAT LOAF

Rock star Meat Loaf admits he doesn't know much about fishing. He just hires a guide and does everything he tells him to do. Well, *almost* everything. He doesn't relinquish his fishing rod, for instance.

While in Miami recording an album in 1982, Marvin Lee Aday, better known as Meat Loaf, wanted to catch a sailfish, so he chartered a boat.

On a flat-calm ocean, they witnessed a sailfish playing with an aluminum can by batting it up into the air with its bill and chasing it. The playful sailfish was not in a biting mood, however. Neither were any of its buddies.

Nothing seemed to work to catch any sailfish, so the skipper suggested trying for sharks. Since it was slow, Meat Loaf agreed, unaware of the battle that lay ahead.

"We were trolling around, moving slow and I got something," Meat Loaf recalls. "He said, 'If you feel something, pull that hook.' So I'm pulling the hook, and we're fighting and fighting. This went on for hours and hours.

"The guy had had a boat down on the Great Barrier Reef and had caught four or five Great White Sharks. He'd shown us pictures of this one great white that he caught that was bigger than the boat he had. So this guy was thinking we'd hooked a great white. He was maneuvering his boat, he was breaking out the guns, they're scrambling.

"When we got it to a certain point, you could see an outline of the shark and it was *huge*. The guy was freaking out. He said, 'Let some line out, let some line out!' He's screaming at me. He's going, 'Let me take this.' I said, 'No, this is my fish. I paid for this, I'm bringing him up. When I get him close enough, you shoot him.'

"So he's freaking out and he's moving the boat, and they're loading these big guns. It was like *Jaws*, right?

"Well, about four-and-a-half hours into the fight, we found out what it was. I had hooked a nine-foot hammerhead and I got him in the side. I had been pulling him up sideways. So you got a thing coming up sideways that looks like it's a nine-foot mouth.

"Everybody was cracking up."

The fish weighed close to 300 pounds. A fiberglass replica of the shark was made and Meat Loaf has it hanging on his wall, a reminder of the day he hooked "Jaws."

Chapter Eight

Presidential Cast

Even the president of the United States needs some time on the water once in a while. The economy, national security and foreign policy are but a few of the storm clouds that can hang over the head of a president, stretching his nerves as tight as 30-pound monofilament pulled taut by a tuna.

For many presidents over the years, fishing was the perfect elixir to calm the political waters storming inside their veins.

Herbert Hoover, one of the many fishing presidents, was vocal about the value of the sport, the character it builds and the balm it provides for stress.

"When all the routines and details and the human bores get on our nerves, we just yearn to go away from here to somewhere else," Hoover

President Herbert Hoover often said fishing washes a man's soul.
He was also fond of saying, "All men are equal before fish."
Photo courtesy of the Herbert Hoover Presidential Library

said in a 1951 speech. "To go fishing is a sound, a valid and an accepted reason for an escape. It requires no explanation."

President Jimmy Carter often used this escape hatch while in office, his fishing trips increasing with each year in office. Coincidence?

From the president's daily diary, the Jimmy Carter Library compiled a list of Carter's fishing trips. They numbered 54 over his four-year term, including 27 trips in his fourth year.

After losing his reelection bid, Carter was said to have gone fishing to salve his wounds.

President George Bush probably fished as much as Carter while in office. He loved to fish and didn't much care if he caught anything. Being outdoors seemed to be what counted most. Addressing a Boy

Scout Jamboree in 1989, Bush spoke about fishing being his favorite form of relaxation.

"It's with a rod and reel that I tend to count my blessings, especially if I'm out there with one of our grandkids or with Barbara, the only woman on earth who can read and fish at the same time—and catch every word and every fish."

Bush and Carter were probably the most prolific presidential anglers over the past 45 years. Their fishing exploits are well chronicled by the media. Yet evidence of fishing presidents dates to the father of our country, George Washington, and suggests several presidents were avid anglers.

Biographies indicate Washington's love for fishing came from the banks of the Rappahannock River in Virginia, and that he enjoyed duck hunting and sturgeon fishing. He was also a commercial shad fisherman.

A large boulder sitting in the Potomac River near the Woodmont Rod and Gun Club north of Washington D.C. is still called Cleveland Rock after President Grover Cleveland, who used to visit the exclusive club and stand on that very rock to fish.

One biography of President Chester Arthur described his "near obsession with fishing." He was the first president to visit Jackson Hole, Wyoming, to fish for trout.

President Ronald Reagan once described in a speech how the Secret Service introduced President Calvin Coolidge to fishing and it became his passion. Reagan said Coolidge, in response to a question from a reporter, estimated his favorite fishing spot held up to 45,000 fish and stated, "I haven't caught them all yet, but I've intimidated them."

Bill Mares, author of *Fishing with the Presidents*, said he uncovered stories about John Quincy Adams, Martin Van Buren and Abraham Lincoln having fished, but none indicated a sustained interest in fishing.

"You could assume if presidents were American boys, they probably all fished a little bit some time along the line," Mares said.

But he found the most avid fishing presidents, aside from Carter and Bush, to be Arthur, Cleveland, Warren Harding, Hoover, Franklin D. Roosevelt and Dwight D. Eisenhower. Like his father, George W. Bush also has fishing in his blood.

Perhaps Roosevelt best epitomized fishing as a stress reliever while in office. Roosevelt took a dose of stress relief prior to the outbreak of World War II.

In *A Rendezvous with Destiny*, Roosevelt is described as fearing that he would have to cancel his fishing vacation aboard the *USS Tuscaloosa* because war was so near. But when told the outbreak of war was a week to 10 days away, Roosevelt replied, "Oh, in that case I really have a couple of weeks to get a rest."

He went fishing off the coast of Labrador and was kept informed of escalating tensions via cables. From his boat, he sent appeals to Germany, Italy and Poland to work out a peaceful resolution. One wonders, if Roosevelt had had his druthers, would he have preferred to continue fishing rather than return to the White House and a world war?

Fishing can help reduce stress but can't totally erase the haunting memories of war. Neal Taylor of Santa Barbara found that out when he fished with President Eisenhower in the early 1960s.

Taylor won a national spin-casting championship while in the air force. Eisenhower heard about it and invited him to go fishing on the Platte River in Colorado.

"I was scared to death," Taylor recalls. "But five minutes after I met the man, I felt like I knew him forever. It was an incredible experience for me."

Indelibly deposited in his memory bank is one particular incident from that trip. As they fished, Eisenhower suddenly stopped and took a seat on the river's edge with elbow on knee and hand on forehead. Taylor thought he had fallen ill.

"Ike, what's wrong?" a concerned Taylor asked.

Eisenhower shook his head side to side and looked up at Taylor and replied, "Neal, there's not a day that goes by that I don't think about the men that lost their lives in Normandy."

Like Taylor, many anglers were fortunate to have fished with presidents over the years and cherish the recollections.

Curt Gowdy, known best for his work as host of *American Sportsman*, remembers salmon fishing with President Carter and the first lady on the Matapedia River in Quebec in early 1980.

As Carter enjoyed some solitude elsewhere on the river, Rosalynn Carter, an adept fly fisher, was filmed catching a 26-pound salmon with some help from Gowdy.

"As she was playing the fish, the reel dropped off her rod and into the river," Gowdy recalls. "It was only four or five feet deep there, and I jumped into the water and retrieved the reel."

As the first lady applied pressure with the rod tip, Gowdy called to the camera crew to toss him a roll of duct tape. He managed to reconnect the reel to the rod while Rosalynn fought the fish. Finally she was able to reel in the fish.

"We got up to the bank to take some pictures," Gowdy says. "I'll never forget it. She looked down and she said, 'And only one broken fingernail.'"

Another episode of the *American Sportsman* featured President Bush and the pursuit of bonefish in the Florida Keys. Gowdy knew it was hopeless as soon as they left the dock. Seven or eight boats loaded with Secret Service, medical staff and rescue personnel escorted the president to the fishing spot.

"We got out there on these flats and these bonefish are really spooky—you can't make a noise or anything—and here's this fleet of boats, and helicopters overhead," Gowdy recalls. "I turned to Bush and said, 'Mr. President, we ain't going to get any fish today.' He laughed and said, 'I think you're right.' We never saw a fish."

Bush spent six hours fishing—without a bite.

One of the best examples of how much Bush enjoys fishing comes from Guy Eaker, a professional bass angler from Cherryville, North Carolina.

Eaker and fellow pro Charlie Ingram were paired to fish with Bush in a 1992 fund-raiser put on by Ray Scott, founder of the Bass Anglers Sportsman Society and its tournament trail.

They were fishing on President's Lake in Alabama, Scott's private lake, when Bush hooked into a feisty three-pound largemouth bass. As Bush went to grab the fish by the lip, it leaped up and nailed Bush with the second treble hook, plunging it deep into his left index finger between the tip and first joint.

"He's hollering and screaming and running around the back of the boat," Eaker recalls. "I took off to the back of the boat. I finally got hold of the fish and got the fish off, and the hook was way down in his index finger."

"What am I going to do?" Bush asked.

"Mr. President, I can get that hook out," Eaker replied.

"You can?"

"I've taken a lot of hooks out of a lot of people. ... I can get it out, but I'm going to have to push it through."

"Well, let's go for it."

Bush knew, as did Eaker, that if his personal physician reached him and saw the embedded hook, he'd be whisked off to the hospital and his day of fishing would be done.

Eaker needed to hurry. The Secret Service and the physician, in a boat nearby, were headed their way upon seeing the commotion.

"I've got a pair of big needlenose pliers and rammed the hook through the skin," Eaker recalls. "He did have about three good choice words when I did that. But I clipped off the barb and brought it back through the finger, and he was bleeding like crazy."

The physician treated the wound and instantly stemmed the bleeding. So Bush continued his day on the water, thanks to Eaker. No way would the physician have attempted to take the hook out of the president, Eaker said. And no way did Bush want to stop fishing.

"I think he was sort of embarrassed and didn't want to have it all over the world that the president had a hook in him and had to be taken to the hospital to get it out," Eaker said.

Another time, Scott had invited the then-vice-president Bush to attend the renowned Bassmaster Classic in Pine Bluff, Arkansas. Bush agreed but expressed a desire to fish while he was there.

So Scott arranged a fishing trip to a small lake on the nearby private ranch of Casey Jones. A few days before Bush's arrival, Scott and some associates fished the pond to test the fishing.

"We fished our tails off and didn't get a bite," Scott said. "It was a pretty little lake, but it wasn't worth a toot."

Scott doesn't recall whose idea it was, but since the classic was catch and release, as was the two media days before the tournament, it was decided the bass would not be released back into the Arkansas River. Instead, they were stocked into Casey Jones's lake.

Bush enjoyed a fine afternoon of bass fishing on Casey Jones's lake before the state fisheries department seined the lake to retrieve the bass and put them back into the river.

"He would have died if he'd known this," Scott said. "I didn't want him to know—and he never did know—that those fish were in fact on a detour trip.

"If George Bush reads this, he will know this for the first time."

Sorry, Mr. President.

Of course, not catching fish might not have mattered much to Bush. As Hoover said, and Bush would probably agree, it isn't the fish that counts. It's the whole experience.

"It is the chance to wash one's soul with pure air, with the rush of the brook or with the shimmer of the sun on blue water," Hoover said in the 1951 speech. "It brings meekness and inspiration from the decency of nature, charity toward tackle makers, patience toward fish, a mockery of profits and egos, a quieting of hate, a rejoicing that you do not have to decide a darned thing until next week. And it is discipline in the equality of men—for all men are equal before fish. And the contemplation of the water, the forest and mountains soothes our troubles, shames our wickedness and inspires us to esteem our fellow men—especially other fishermen."

GEORGE BUSH

As President George Bush climbed into his boat for another day of fishing, the media peppered him with questions in hopes of a sound bite.

His answer about the Poland Parliament appointing a new prime minister was pure vanilla, as were his other retorts.

Finally, one reporter broached the topic that hardly mattered to national security but was of great importance to those covering the president's vacation.

"Mr. President," the reporter said, allowing the statement to act as a question, "America is worried about the fishing."

"So am I," Bush replied with a quip. "If you'd keep your damn boats away from me, I could catch some!"

One week into a three-week vacation in August 1989 off Kennebunkport, Maine, Bush had produced nary a bluefish and the president had fished every day. The pressure was mounting, and the media was starting to run with the story, which grew bigger with each fishless day.

Making things worse, an 18-pound bluefish was caught from an ABC-TV camera boat, prompting Bush to say: "There's no justice here. That's not fair."

The press agreed to a truce on the ninth day. They would keep their chase boats farther away to give Bush space and prevent fish from being spooked off.

But it didn't matter. Bush went without a fish again.

On the 10th day of his vacation, Bush took Reverend Billy Graham with him. The headline in the *Maine Sunday Telegram* the next day told the story: "President comes back empty handed again."

Ever hopeful, Bush told the press, "We'll get some. I'd like it recorded on CNN."

Bush needn't have worried. With seemingly every major media outlet covering his bad-luck fishing, one TV network was sure to capture the moment. As soon as he caught a bluefish, the world would know.

In the meantime, the *Portland Press Herald*, a local newspaper, began running a daily box score called "Fish watch" that had a bluefish in a circle with a slash through it, indicating no fish. "President Bush has now gone on 11 outings without catching a fish," one update read.

Newspapers across the country reportedly asked the *Portland Press Herald* to fax them the "Fish watch" box score each day. Joking during one news briefing—at least it was presumed he was kidding—Bush called the logo a "vicious assault on my ability."

"I think they should knock off that advertisement on the front of the Portland paper that shows a bluefish with a big X (read: slash) through it," he said.

As with his fishing, Bush didn't have any luck in convincing the paper not to run the embarrassing box score.

Just as people come out of the woodwork with suggestions for baseball players in batting slumps, veteran anglers were quick to offer the president advice.

These experts were quoted in *USA Today* and local newspapers. If they didn't offer a tip, they expressed sympathy for his not catching any fish.

"It's gotten out of hand," Bush told reporters with Canadian prime minister Brian Mulroney at his side. "When I see it on national television, I know I've got to put an end to this monkey business.

"Between now and when I leave on Monday, I guarantee you—I positively guarantee you—that this jinx will be broken. I've seen a lot of good .350 hitters bat about .178 for a while. Then they come out of the slump and move forward.

"My record fishing in these waters is well known. It's a superb record—a record of bountiful catches, and somehow, some things have gone wrong for the last 13 days, something's happened."

The next day, this newfound confidence resulted in the president catching...nothing. "Day 14 and still no fish," a story in the *Portland Press Herald* began.

Photographers began wearing t-shirts that read, "Presidential Fish Watch: Kennebunkport 1989." On the dock, family members chanted "We want fish" and "Go for the blues," and sang, "When the fish go marching in."

They also held up signs as the president departed on another fishing trip. One said, "Fish till you drop." Another: "A fish a day keeps the press away."

On the 15th outing, Bush caught a four-inch pollack but refused to call an end to the streak.

"Not until we get a bluefish," he said. "We've got to go for the blues."

Sixteenth outing: No bluefish.

Seventeenth outing: No bluefish.

Time was running out. Two more days of vacation remained. Two more chances to catch a bluefish.

"This is it! I can feel it," Bush said before attending church services. "We're going out the minute church is over."

Wearing a hat with "USS Bluefish" lettering, Bush vowed to stay out "as long as it takes" to get one and commenced fishing.

And on that Sabbath Day, whether it was Divine intervention or the moon being aligned with Mars, Bush finally put his hook into a 10-pound bluefish.

When the fish was gaffed and brought on board, Bush's son Marvin raised his father's arm above his head, signaling the new heavyweight champion fisherman of the world.

Horns blared. On-lookers yelled. Presses were stopped. A White House aide broadcasted the news over a network of pagers worn by dozens of reporters: "The president caught a blue at 11:30 this morning. Details to follow."

A *New York Times* reporter wrote that the mood resembled election night 1988 when the *Fidelity*, the president's boat, roared into Walker's Point with Bush holding up his fish. The excitement was overwhelming.

"The jinx is broken!" Bush proclaimed.

The president fulfilled his promise to catch a fish. Not his greatest landing, Bush admitted, but a catch nonetheless.

"I saw a bunch of birds and started to reel in, and wham," Bush said, explaining how he caught the most celebrated bluefish in history.

"It's been a long, dry summer, but it all worked out. This is icing on the cake."

Finally, the *Portland Press Herald* removed the slash from its "Fish watch" logo, reporting, "After at least 17 outings, President Bush finally caught a bluefish Sunday."

As the president cleaned the fish on the rocks, he was asked why he didn't stuff the fish.

"Stuff it?" he replied in an awkward sound bite, "we were lucky to catch it."

The next day, the final day of his vacation, Bush went fishing again. The excitement of the previous day had been washed away. The anticipation was nonexistent. The hoopla wilted. The media circus had taken down their tents.

This time, Bush landed two bluefish, each weighing more than 10 pounds—and hardly anyone noticed. To the media and the world, it was just another day of fishing.

RICHARD NIXON

President Dwight D. Eisenhower, an avid fisherman, once tried teaching his vice-presidential running mate Richard Nixon how to cast with a fly rod.

Nixon's first cast hooked a tree limb. His second cast hooked a tree limb. His third cast hooked a tree limb. His fourth cast hooked Eisenhower's shirt.

"The lesson ended abruptly," Nixon wrote in his book, *In the Arena*. "I could see that he was disappointed because he loved fishing and could not understand why others did not like it as well as he did."

Clearly, as Eisenhower discovered, Nixon was not a born fisherman.

When Nixon was a teenager, he once tried deep-sea fishing but gave it up due to seasickness.

"Fishing," Nixon wrote, "just isn't my bag."

FRANKLIN D. ROOSEVELT

You don't always need a hook to catch a fish. President Franklin D. Roosevelt proved that on a trip to Cocos Island where he landed a 100-pound sailfish without a hook.

As he often did, FDR shared the fish story during a press conference at Hyde Park, New York on August 27, 1938. He said there were 11 witnesses on the boat and "a moving picture camera," plus two other cameras to verify the story.

"We were out fishing, trolling for sailfish," he recalled. "One of them took my line, which was out about 200 feet beyond the boat with a hook and feather on the end.

"He jumped in the air and, apparently, while he was on the end, another sailfish came along and got his beak all snarled up in the line. The fish that got caught on the hook got away, but the fish that got caught on his nose was hauled in."

HERBERT HOOVER

A White House tradition for years before President Herbert Hoover took office in 1929 was for a local fishing club to present the president with its first salmon of the season.

The president would pose with the fish for photos that would adorn the club's walls.

Hoover, one of this country's most avid presidential anglers, upheld the tradition. Unfortunately, his new secretary wasn't clear on the ritual.

"Where is the salmon?" Hoover asked the secretary.

"I sent it to the White House kitchen," the secretary replied.

The secretary was sent to the kitchen to save the salmon only to find the cook had chopped off the head and tail and was ready to cook it. Oops.

Fortunately, the chef cooked up a tradition-saving recipe. He stuffed the fish with cotton and sewed the head and tail back on. The secretary brought the fish out to the White House lawn and told Hoover to hold the fish horizontally because of its fragile state.

The president held the fish for the photographers, one of whom whispered to Hoover that something was wrong. A piece of cotton was sticking out of the fish.

In Herbert Hoover: A Biography, *Hoover is said to have written
in a magazine article, "Fisherman are always good company.
They are optimistic or they would not be fishermen."*
Photo courtesy of the Herbert Hoover Presidential Library

"A president must be equal to emergencies," Hoover wrote in his
book, *FISHING FOR FUN—And to Wash Your Soul.*

"I carefully held up the fish with my hand over the spot of cotton.
The directors of the fishing club, the fish and I posed before 20 photographers—and each posed for 'Just one more' six times. But the cotton
kept oozing out of the fish as was proved by the later photographs. The
fishing club did not use those later editions."

JIMMY CARTER

The most celebrated fishing story in the history of the White House
is the one about how the *presidency* got away.

On April 20, 1979, president Jimmy Carter was fishing from a canoe on his farm pond in Plains, Georgia, when an enraged rabbit began swimming toward him.

Apparently, it had designs on getting into the canoe with Carter and attacking him. Without Secret Service anywhere near his canoe, Carter's only defense was to use his paddle to ward off the hissing, menacing creature.

When Carter returned to the White House and his staff heard what happened, they didn't believe it. Rabbits don't swim and if they did, they don't attack U.S. presidents.

As proof, Carter produced a photo taken by a White House photographer, showing him with raised paddle fighting off something in the water. Still the staff was doubtful. So Carter had the photograph enlarged. It purportedly was the wild hare.

Sometime later, before the Democratic Convention, White House press secretary Jody Powell inexplicably leaked the story to Brooks Jackson of the Associated Press and the rabbit, so to speak, was out of the bag.

Suddenly, Carter needed more than a paddle to stave off a wave of skepticism and comments about the president fighting a rabid rabbit.

"It was a fairly robust-looking rabbit who was swimming, apparently with no difficulty," Carter told reporters, adding that had the animal gotten into the canoe it would have been "an unpleasant situation for me and the rabbit."

Carter told *ABC News* correspondent Sam Donaldson, "Rabbits swim and that one was swimming without any difficulty at all. I can certify to that."

The story became front-page news. The "Banzai Bunny" or "Killer Rabbit" were hot topics on Capital Hill. Columnists enjoyed a field day as Carter became the butt of countless jokes.

Some feel Carter, whose popularity was already waning, destroyed whatever chance he had left for reelection because of the negative publicity about the rabbit, which became the most celebrated bunny since Bugs.

To this day, the incident has stuck with the president like glue. At least he maintains a sense of humor. At the Carter Administration 20-

year reunion in 1997, Carter reportedly was presented with a broken oar and a giant stuffed animal, presumably a rabbit. He laughed.

"After writing my Carter biography," author Douglas Brinkley told *ABC News* columnist Buck Wolf, "I can tell you, more people ask about the bunny than about the Camp David Accord or the Panama Canal Treaty. Strange."

Chapter Nine

Memorable Moments

The moment is golden and sticks to the memory bank like adhesive, never to be forgotten. It is the catch of a lifetime that is gaffed, netted, dragged to shore or scooped up in bare hands. Or maybe it is a fishing trip with someone special or an unexpected encounter with nature.

These mental snapshots mark a time and place for anglers the way people know where they were when man first walked on the moon. The instant is frozen in time.

It was the summer of 1972. I was 17. I landed a 20-pound king salmon fishing with my uncle and dad in Washington. The fish broke the calm surface with a swirl, announcing its presence as we trolled by. Next thing you know, my rod dipped and the fight was on. ...

Anglers retell fishing tales a million times or as often as *M*A*S*H* reruns are shown on television. It is as much a part of fishing as landing the fish in the first place.

One age-old story that is retold to this day is about a catch of a lifetime that any avid bass angler would envy. If they don't know the tale, they most likely recognize the name of the angler: George Washington Perry.

On June 2, 1932, Perry landed what has become the most coveted fishing record in history. His 22-pound, 4-ounce largemouth bass caught at Montgomery Lake, Georgia, is the world record.

Perry, a pilot, died in a plane crash in 1974, yet his story and record seem to grow in stature with every year that passes without someone catching a bigger bass.

"The longer it goes, the longer it's on the books, the more hallowed it becomes," said Mike Leech, former president of the International Game Fish Association, the keeper of world records.

"I'm sure for the first 10 or 20 years it wasn't nearly as hallowed. People thought, 'Yeah, it was a big fish, but somebody's going to catch a bigger one.' Nobody paid too much attention to it. But then over the years, as more articles have been written about it and more references made to it, it gets bigger and bigger in the history of fishing."

Millionaire status is said to await the angler who catches the world record. Endorsements and speaking engagements are sure to follow. Before his death, Perry guessed that the fish would be worth $10,000 had he caught it in 1974.

What would Perry have thought about all the ruckus made about the record nowadays?

"He would laugh at it good naturedly," said Bill Baab, an outdoors writer in Georgia who is an historian on Perry and the record. "He could never figure out why all the excitement. ... He didn't deem the fish of any importance. He always had that expression of, 'Gosh, all this about a fish?'"

The bass-fishing community, obviously, views it differently. The fish is legendary, the story one for the ages.

Perry was one of six kids who lived on a farm with his mother. His father passed away the year before and Perry became the family breadwinner.

The depression was in full swing when fishing history was made. Perry, 19 at the time, worked the family farm. But on that day in June 1932, nasty weather prevented him from working the fields. So Perry and a friend, Jack Page, decided to go fishing. Conditions couldn't have been worse. Rain and wind were constant companions.

They went to Montgomery Lake where the john boat Perry had made was pulled up onto shore. The lake was an oxbow off the Ocmulgee River and was filled with tree stumps and Cypress knees.

With only one fishing rod and one lure, a Creek Chub Wiggle Fish, Perry and Page traded off fishing and rowing.

The fishing was slow. Then suddenly a big fish struck. A moment later, the line snapped, and the fish and lure were lost. They sat dejected in disbelief. Their day was over, they thought. A few minutes later, a chain pickerel thrashed its head on the surface and threw the plug. They scooped the lure off the surface, retied it to the 24-pound-test line and were back in business.

Near the end of the day, they noticed a swirl in the water, a telltale sign of a fish near the surface. So Perry tossed the plug in its direction and started working it.

"I don't remember many details, but all at once the water splashed everywhere," Perry told *Sports Afield* in 1969. "I do remember striking, then raring back and trying to reel. But nothing budged. I thought sure I'd lost the fish, that he'd dived and hung me up. I had no idea how big the fish was, but that didn't matter. What had me worried was losing the lure. It was the only one we had between us."

In an interview with *BASSMaster* magazine in 1974, Perry recalled a rather uneventful fight.

"A fish of that size isn't too spectacular in the water, just heavy and cumbersome," he said. "I didn't want to pressure him on that line. The bass did work its way into a half-submerged tree top, but finally it tired of my constant pressure, and I got him in."

A world record was the last thing on Perry's mind as the pair rowed to shore and headed for the town of Helena.

"When I caught that 22-pounder, the first thing I thought of was how nice a chunk of meat to take home," he told *Sports Afield*. "It was almost an accident that I had it weighed and recorded. It created a lot of attention that day in Helena."

He took it to show friends at the general store where somebody suggested he should enter *Field and Stream* magazine's Big Fish Contest. Entering required weighing the fish on a certified scale. So Perry took the fish to the post office where it was certified by the postmaster. The fish measured 32.5 inches with a girth of 28.5 inches. The weight of 22-4 will forever be associated with Perry, though at the time it was just a big fish.

"I never even thought about mounting it or even taking a picture," Perry said in *Sports Afield*. "I just took the fish home and we ate it."

Perry won the contest and received a $75 gift certificate with which he used to obtain an automatic shotgun, shells, rod and reel, and outdoor clothing.

Two years later, he caught a 13-pound, 14-ounce largemouth bass, entered the contest again and won another $75 gift certificate, which was akin to winning a lottery in those days.

Perry didn't learn until considerably later that his fish was a world record. He didn't much care about that, though. He was clearly most pleased about the contest winnings.

The IGFA was founded in 1939 and starting keeping world records, but it wasn't until the late 1960s that the record largemouth bass started becoming a big deal.

"Other magazines mentioned the record from time to time, but it didn't really become significant in the minds of a lot of folks until B.A.S.S. was organized and started getting members," Baab said.

The formation of the Bass Anglers Sportsman Society, founded by Ray Scott, began in 1967 with its first tournament. Bass fishing took off, and today largemouth bass is the most popular freshwater gamefish in the U.S.

Anglers pursue the world record as if it is the Holy Grail. The record has been threatened a few times over the years but remains up for grabs.

Perhaps the closest the record came to falling was the alleged 24-pounder caught by Paul Duclos in Spring Lake in Sonoma County, California, in March 1997. The photo of Duclos holding the behemoth bass makes for a compelling argument as to the weight of the fish. However, Duclos opted to release the fish alive back into the lake before it could be certified by proper fish-and-game personnel.

Worse, Duclos weighed the fish on a bathroom scale, hardly a method the IGFA would ever approve for establishing a record, particularly for such a sacred one as this.

"My position is very simple," B.A.S.S. founder Ray Scott says. "If it's a record, it needs to be killed because that eliminates any prospects of impropriety and also lets everybody see the fish, and it can be examined."

At the very least, the angler who makes this memorable catch must have it verified by proper authorities.

No doubt, the bass of a lifetime is swimming out there someplace. Leech suggests it might be some kid sitting on the bank with a worm who eventually lucks onto the right fish and breaks the record.

"Someday somebody's going to do it," Leech adds, "and God bless them when they do."

ANDY GARCIA

Andy Garcia's fishing buddies laughed as he attached a three-pronged fork to the end of a broomstick.

"What the hell you gonna catch with that thing?" they asked.

"Well," the actor replied, "I'm going to spear some mullet for bait."

As a kid growing up in Miami Beach, Garcia and his friends used this makeshift apparatus to spear mullet from low bridges in the canals near his home. His adult friends weren't buying it, however.

"You'll never spear anything with that," they told him.

A week later, as Garcia waited to go fishing with his fishing buddies, he noticed a huge barracuda hanging out near his backyard dock that fronts a Miami harbor. The fish was hunting for mullet that congregate underneath his dock.

So Garcia grabbed his broomstick.

"It was a sitting duck, really," Garcia recalls. "The barracuda has been eating our bait for years, so I nailed it."

It was definitely a keeper. His catch of a lifetime weighed 48 pounds!

"So when my friends came to fish, I said, 'Look what I caught with my spear.'"

Garcia lifted the fish from a cooler and jaws dropped.

"They couldn't believe it. They had laughed me off the dock just a week earlier with my Miami Beach spear.

"It probably is a world record. It's probably the only one of its kind. I don't think anybody has ever caught a barracuda with a broomstick and a trident head."

BOBBY KNIGHT

For coach Bobby Knight, the fishing trips with his father, two sons and wife are golden moments he treasures as one would a family heirloom. His greatest joy with a fishing rod comes from sharing time on the water with family.

Nothing could be better, in Knight's eyes.

Yet as unforgettable stories go, the one that stands out like neon is the summer trip to Russia in 1991 when he fished for Atlantic salmon with legendary baseball player Ted Williams and legendary fishing-show host Jerry McKinnis.

"I've had a lot of great experiences fishing, but that was as good as they come," Knight says.

Williams was Knight's childhood idol whom he met at a spring training through a mutual friend. McKinnis, well, Knight says he's never met anybody in sports he liked better. Knight has been a featured guest of McKinnis several times on his long-running show *The Fishin' Hole*.

When McKinnis told Knight about the phenomenal Atlantic salmon fishing on the Kola Peninsula in Russia, Knight suggested taking Williams there, knowing his penchant for pursuing and catching Atlantic salmon.

The Splendid Splinter never hesitated when Knight extended the invitation—and the historic trip was on.

"The first day, Ted said, 'OK, let me see your rods,'" Knight remembers.

Knight took three rods with him. He handed him his seven weight. Williams flexed it against the ceiling to see how strong it was.

"Goddam, Coach, these are pretty good, pretty goddam good rods you got here, Coach, kind of surprises me," Williams told him. "Now let me see your reels."

Knight never fly fished for big game, only trout. So he never gave much thought to reels. He saw them only as things to store the line, not reel in the fish.

*Ted Williams and Bobby Knight chat in a helicopter in Russia
as they travel to their fly-fishing destination. Knight called it
"The most memorable fishing trip I imagine that I'll ever have."*
Photo courtesy of Bobby Knight

"So I dump out three or four reels on the table and he looks at it and says, 'This may be the greatest chickenshit collection of junk I've ever seen,'" Knight recalls.

His inferior reels held up fine until Day 3, a spectacular day on which he caught and released an unheard of nine Atlantic salmon. Most ranged from seven to nine pounds, one was 15 to 17 pounds, and the last one was the granddaddy of them all, one he couldn't quite get a handle on—at first.

It was the end of the day and the others had retreated to camp. Knight hooked into a large salmon with his guide, a Russian kid name Sasha, beside him.

Clearly, Knight's inexpensive, green Heddon reel was not up to the task, basically proving that "junk" was an appropriate adjective used by Williams to describe it.

When the fish took off, the fish was "on the reel." In fly-fisher lingo, this means he wasn't just pulling in the line and allowing it to collect in the water around him. He was fighting this fish with the reel.

"I started working it and all of a sudden it took off and the handle on the reel hit my thumb and broke completely off," Knight recalls. "Now, I know I've got a bigger fish than I thought I had and I'm trying to palm the reel to get the line back in."

Attempting to work the reel was tough enough. Having the fish run down river made it more difficult. Knight and Sasha maneuvered around rocks and tree roots, dodged limbs, and followed that fish down river while trying to fight it.

Along the way, Knight, just as quickly as he might come up with a defensive strategy to shut down a hot-shooting team during a basketball game, adapted a method for reeling in the fish without a reel handle.

Knight broke off a small branch and stuck it into a hole on the side of the fly reel. With the impromptu reel handle, he managed to gain line. Clever. Sasha, though he spoke no English, took Knight's cue and began whittling sticks into spare handles. When one would break, Sasha handed Knight another.

After about an hour and a 600-yard run down river, Knight finally corralled the huge salmon in an eddy. Sasha grabbed the line at the leader knot and the fish laid in the water between them. They admired the beautiful creature.

"As he's getting ready to reach down for the fish, the fish slips the hook and just kind of slowly drifts back toward the river," Knight remembers.

It was a perfect release, really. It was too dark for a photo and Knight didn't have a camera to take a picture, anyway.

Sasha told Knight, "11, 12 kilo—11, 12 kilo!" indicating the estimated weight of the fish.

"That translated is a fish that weighs about 25 pounds," Knight says. "That was the most spectacular fish I think I've ever caught. The thing that I thought when it was all said and done was this: Sash and I won because we got to see the fish up close, and the fish won because it slipped the hook in the end. That was a great ending to that fish."

Williams was impressed with Knight's ad lib with the reel handle and probably was a bit ashamed, since he intended to lend Knight a better reel. The last two days, Knight used one of Williams's reels.

All told, they spent five days fishing. Knight hooked 30 salmon and Williams hooked 22, despite fishing a considerably less amount of time than the younger Knight.

"So many things make this memorable," Knight says.

Such as:

• Before the trip, Williams accompanied then-President George Bush on Air Force One to the all-star baseball game in Montreal and told Bush about their upcoming fishing trip to Russia.

"All Bush said was, 'Geez, this may set diplomatic relations back a decade,'" Knight remembers.

• Knight had planned to send a friend in the White House two cards to give to President Bush, one to let him know the trio was on their way and another a week later to say mission accomplished, but he forgot to mail them.

"About a week after we came back was the Russian revolution, when Gorbachev was thrown out and Yeltsin came in. I always thought maybe it was just as well I had forgotten to send the cards."

• Vladimir Kondrashin, the former Russian national basketball team coach and an acquaintance of Knight, set up dinner for the trio in St. Petersburg.

"We went through five or six courses and we were full and tired and sleepy and no longer hungry and, I'll never forget this, we thanked them profusely and left—and we hadn't had the main course yet."

• Knight was tailing a fish caught by Williams, taking the hook out and releasing it for his idol when he asked him a question.

"I said, 'Would you rather catch this fish or hit a home run?' He looked at me and thought for a second. 'I think I'd rather see the ball go in the seats than feel the fish hit the fly, but it's close.'"

• Williams tied two flies for Knight and stuck them on a post outside Knight's cabin. Knight put them in a container to bring home.

"They sit in a statue of him on top of our television set to this day."

• Two Americans back at the lodge suggested a trip the next day to a part of the peninsula that had never been fished. Knight was ready to go with them, but McKinnis talked him out of it.

"It was the next day that I caught the nine fish. I kissed Jerry after the day was over. He still laughs about that."

• On the flight home, Knight was half asleep when he heard Williams talking to a passenger beside him. The passenger, assuming Knight was asleep, asked Williams what kind of guy Knight was.

"This may be the nicest thing I ever heard anybody say about me," Knight recalls. "Ted said, 'Well, I'll tell you this: The sonafabitch is just like me.'"

It was icing for the once-in-a-lifetime experience, one Knight will never tire of retelling.

"The best fishing partners have been those four people in my family," Knight said of his father, sons and wife. "But this is the most memorable fishing trip I imagine that I'll ever have."

CHARLTON HESTON

Fishing never interested Charlton Heston like hunting did. The actor would much rather have a rifle in his hands than a fishing rod.

So perhaps it is understandable that Heston's most memorable fishing experience was one in which he used a primitive method for catching fish.

As a kid growing up in Michigan, he went spearfishing for pike through the ice.

At a hunting convention in the late 1990s, Heston revealed the tactics:

A shanty was towed by truck to a spot on the ice. It was equipped with a stove, benches and a square opening in the floor where a large hole in the ice was made.

Hand-carved wooden fish, about eight inches long and filled with lead, were used for bait. They were dropped into the water with string. To attract pike, the baits were moved in figure-eights. Soon, the dark shape of a pike would appear through the translucent water.

As if hunting, Heston lunged at the fish with a six-foot spear with three prongs, impaling the fish. He said it was easier than you'd think.

Keeping the catch fresh was pretty easy, too.

"When you spear something, you just open the door and throw it out on the ice and it freezes instantly because it gets pretty cold up there," Heston explained.

"That's the only fishing I got much fun out of. I've fished in the gulf and off Hawaii and that's exciting, of course, but fishing is not really my sport. My son is a fly fisherman. He loves fly fishing. I realize fly fishing is something of an art. It was just not something that ever appealed to me. Fishing, unlike hunting, is a passive sport. But fishing through the ice in one of those shacks when I was 10 years old was a lot of fun."

OSCAR DE LA HOYA

From the opening bell, Oscar De La Hoya was in trouble. The champion boxer was cut and bleeding, and the fight had barely begun.

The bout took place off the coast of Cabo San Lucas, Baja, in 1997 and the opponent was a blue marlin, a heavyweight in any fisherman's book.

"I was out on the deck of the boat getting a suntan," the champ recalls. "All of a sudden, I heard the reel: 'Zzzzzz.'

"'Oh man, we got something!' So I got up and was going to the rail to the rod. First, I slice my finger: 'Shooo.' I thought my finger was going to fall off. It wouldn't stop bleeding.

"Then, still running because I was excited, I hit my toe on something. I don't know what it was, an edge or something. And I sliced that, too.

"So I was bleeding from the finger and I was bleeding from my little toe, and I was still excited because the reel was still going, 'Zzzzzz.' I was running and running and going to the line and then I fell over. Still, I didn't care what pain I was feeling.

"Finally I got there, bleeding, hurt, and I was there for an hour and a half just reeling it in."

As he sat in the fighting chair battling this bruiser, his handlers were attending to his wounds.

"They were wrapping me up and everything while I was bringing the fish in," De La Hoya says. "It was exciting."

Excruciating, too. Or was it?

"You know what?" he says. "The adrenaline was pumping so fast I didn't feel it. Actually, it was like a fight. I didn't feel no pain. I was excited, I was nervous, I was thinking, 'Man, what if this guy gets away?'

"After an hour, I was thinking, 'Gosh, if he gets away, he knocked me out.'"

But it was a bruised and battered De La Hoya that was victorious over that 210-pound blue marlin.

Unlike his other fight victims, De La Hoya stuffed and mounted this one on the wall to serve as a reminder of the bloody battle he endured.

"That baby got me," he says.

ALICE COOPER

Alice Cooper enjoyed the performance of a lifetime on a sandy stage in Cabo San Lucas in June of 1996. Cooper was rock and reelin' to the tune of big roosterfish.

Cooper had only fished a couple times before a local guide, Jeff Klassen, asked if he wanted to try surf fishing. He said sure.

"There were about 10 of us," recalls Cooper, who was in Cabo rehearsing for a tour and to play golf. "He got us those big poles and everything. I had never surf fished before. These 12- to 14-foot waves would come in. Right at the top, the waves would be clear and you'd see huge fish weighing 45, 60 pounds. All you'd have to do is hit the top of the wave with your lure and they'd go right at it.

"We had 20 fish in one hour, releasing them all since they're not good to eat.

"Every time you'd look there was somebody reeling one in. My son, Dash, he'd catch one and they'd start pulling him into the water. He caught a 65-pounder and it took four of us to hold. That was a great day for Dash. He caught a 65-pound fish and had a hole-in-one playing golf. It was like the best day of his life."

It was for guide Klassen, too.

"We must have caught them in some kind of feeding frenzy or something," Cooper continues. "The guide said, 'I've never seen it like this before. This is unbelievable.' We just figured this happens every day."

Cooper and his angling entourage soon learned, however, that fishing doesn't always rock and roll.

"The next day," Cooper says, "we went out for snapper on the Pacific side and we didn't catch anything."

Rock star Alice Cooper, more of a golfer than fisherman, hit the jackpot with this nice roosterfish, caught while fishing the surf of Cabo San Lucas in 1996.
Photo by Mike Meadows

NOLAN RYAN

Nolan Ryan, known for his 100 mph fastballs, packed more than heat when he and the California Angels took off on a road trip in the early 1970s.

"We'd take our fishing poles with us," the Hall of Fame pitcher said. "If we had an off day in Cleveland, we'd fish in some of those private lakes in the area or Milwaukee or Kansas City—wherever we could find places.

"If you spent an off day on the road, you were looking for something to do. For us, to get away from the hotel and the crowds, it was real relaxing to get out and fish somewhere."

So five or six times a year, fishing rod cases could be seen with the baseball equipment coming down the airport luggage carrier. The rods belonged to Ryan and his teammates/fishing partners Ken Berry and Tom Mcraw.

Occasionally a rubber snake was part of the baggage of Ryan or Berry. As they fished along the shore, one of them would place the snake in the path of McCraw.

"Tom McCraw was extremely scared of snakes," Ryan said. "So we'd usually try to at least scare him one trip. He was pretty leery of us and was always anticipating something and stayed on his guard."

On a really good day, the snakes left them alone and they would catch 25 to 30 bass, releasing most if not all of them.

"What we did sometimes, if we had a good day, we would take some of the fish back, clean 'em and let the clubhouse guy fry 'em up, which was kind of a treat," Ryan said. "It was kind of pregame appetizers."

GARY CHAPMAN

Once an angler loses a fish, it's usually gone for good. There's no catching the one that got away. So how remarkable was it for Gary Chapman to catch five that got away?

Chapman, a Christian music artist and former host of *Prime Time Country* on TNN, was 12 or 13 when he was enjoying a great day of bass fishing on a friend's pond in De Leon, Texas.

Hall of Fame pitcher Nolan Ryan poses with one of his catches on Fox Sports Southwest Outdoors *a series of fishing and hunting shows Ryan hosts.*
Photo courtesy of FSN Southwest

"I caught five that I was really proud of from two to four pounds, but I didn't bring a stringer," he says. "So I cut a little willow branch and had them all jammed down in the mud at the edge of the pond to keep them in the water until I was ready to go.

"I was getting ready to leave and they were gone. The branch had worked its way out of the mud and I had lost them all. I was heartbroken. I was thinking, 'What a waste. Oh well, I had fun anyway.'

"I was just casting away, no thoughts. I needed to leave but made one more cast, and dang if I didn't snag that branch that was swimming along the top of the water out in the middle of the pond.

"I snagged that branch and I caught five nice bass at one time."

MARCUS ALLEN

Marcus Allen held up the catch of a lifetime and posed for a snapshot, exposing a smile as artificial as a hand-tied fly.

This was a trophy fish, a 30-pound king salmon, a fish any angler would envy. Indeed, it was fishing's equivalent to the Heisman Trophy, NFL MVP or Super Bowl MVP—trophies Allen can relate to.

So why didn't he seem excited? Why the indifferent look in what would be a keepsake photograph? Truth is, Allen didn't make this catch. His wife, Kathryn, did.

The couple was fishing out of Anchorage, Alaska, where trophy-sized king salmon eluded Allen much like he eluded tacklers throughout his storied football career. It was the opposite for Kathryn, who caught fish after trophy fish on that trip in June of 1996.

Every morning they'd take off in a helicopter to various rivers to catch 30-pound salmon and the story would repeat itself. Kathryn would catch fish and Allen would not.

"I got about four on my line and they all got away," Allen says. "So what I did was, in case I didn't catch any in the next couple of days, I took a picture..."

"With my fish," Kathryn quickly adds.

"Just in case," Allen explains, "so I could go back home and tell everybody what a great day I had.

"Well, the second day went by, the same thing happened. I got about four, maybe five on my line. You could see them jumping out of

Marcus Allen has won a lot of trophies in football, but this king salmon caught in Alaska was one of his biggest trophies in fishing.
Photo courtesy of Marcus Allen

the water. Huge! This was my first time king salmon fishing, and they all got off. They either snapped my line or spit the hook."

He fought one for 20 minutes only to lose it. Kathryn and the guide agonized for Allen. She says it was like death when he'd lose a fish and that they were ready to jump into the river and grapple hook a fish for him if they had to.

Time was running out. Allen—0 for two days and soon to be skunked on the final day, as well—hooked up one more time. Only an hour remained before they were to head home. Finally—thankfully!—Allen scored, and in a big way.

"I always say, 'Don't worry, I'm going to catch the biggest fish,'" Allen says. "Well, I cast it out there and the next thing I know, I hooked him. I'd give him room to run and it'd get tired and I'd bring it back in and back up to shore because you had to keep it away from the rocks. These are all the things I learned. I'd walk back out there into the river and let it get tired a little bit more. Then I'd reel him in and pull back and get him away from the rocks. Next thing I know, it's only five feet away. Finally, he comes up and HE...IS...HUGE.

The fish was so big, Allen fumbled it once before recovering and finally getting the photo snapped.

"I had him in two hands when I took the picture—smiling," he says.

The fish, the biggest of the trip, weighed 50 pounds. Allen's smile, also the trip's biggest, stretched 50 yards.

"He looked like a kid in a candy store," Kathryn says. "When he took the picture with my fish, it was like the phoniest smile. You could just tell his heart was hurting him. Then, when he finally brought one in, his smile was ear to ear. It was just huge. Then it was OK to go home."

For Allen, another trophy had been added to his collection.

WAYNE GRETZKY

The Great One, Wayne Gretzky, is a not-so-great fisherman, this the retired hockey star readily admits. He has gotten far more pucks into a net than fish.

Gretzky doesn't do a whole lot of catching when he goes fishing. Heck, Gretzky doesn't even land a fish in his favorite fishing story, though he does win the jackpot.

Gretzky was fishing outside of Boston in 1984 with ex-hockey players Wayne Cashman and Ace Bailey, a pair of experienced anglers.

"We didn't catch anything and this boat pulled into the dock beside us and they had this great, big, huge tuna that they caught," Gretzky recalls. "So they all threw 20 bucks into the pot. There must have been 20 guys around there, and they were all guessing the weight of the tuna. I've never seen a tuna in my life. Well, the tuna weighed 820 pounds, I guessed 810 and I won the pot."

RANDALL "DUKE" CUNNINGHAM

Randall "Duke" Cunningham, the man the movie *Top Gun* was based on, remembers his most thrilling fishing experience occurred as a 12-year-old.

The Republican Congressman, who grew up in the small town of Shelbina, Missouri, was fishing at Shelbina Lake when he caught an eight-and-a-half-pound largemouth bass.

"I didn't even reel it in," he says. "I just started running backward and drug that baby out of there onto the bank. I walked all the way back into town, which is about four miles, and they took a picture of it."

To this day, Cunningham is proud to say that his fish photo appeared in the Shelbina *Democrat*.

SUGAR RAY LEONARD

Not long after defeating Thomas Hearns in a welterweight unification bout in 1981, Sugar Ray Leonard took on a heavyweight—a swordfish.

OK, maybe the 60-pound swordfish was more like a lightweight by sportfishing standards, but on the light tackle Sugar Ray was using, it was all he could handle during this "bout" in the Florida Keys.

Sugar Ray would pull and reel in some line. The fish would pull and take out some line. This give and take went on repeatedly until it got to the point Sugar Ray was about ready to give up.

"It was such a challenge and it was so exhilarating," he said. "It was like a fight because you're waiting, being patient, thinking about the opportunity, being patient and trying to set him up."

Cheering Sugar Ray on from a corner of the boat were his parents and his trainer at the time, Angelo Dundee, and Dundee's wife. Just like a fight, Sugar Ray said.

"I'll tell you what, I'll never forget that experience," Sugar Ray said. "It was great. It was a lot of work, a lot of work. I exerted so much energy. My muscles were totally exhausted."

The battle ended after 45 minutes when a tired Sugar Ray brought down a tired fish to the canvas. Keeping the fish was not a unanimous decision, however.

"I wanted to just let it go, but Angelo Dundee and my parents were so enthralled by this whole experience, they wanted me to pull it in," Sugar Ray said.

So he did. The fish was mounted and placed over the fireplace at his mother's home in South Carolina.

What nearly KO'd Sugar Ray was the taxidermist's bill.

"It cost more than the fishing trip," he said.

Chapter Ten

The One
That Got Away

You set the hook on a fish. Line peels off the reel. The rod bends under the weight of the fish. Adrenaline shoots through your veins faster than water from a fire hose as you begin to realize the fish is enormous.

With every pump of the rod and turn of the reel, the anticipation builds toward a climax like a good movie.

Oh, boy, this is a big one. Could be a record. It might be big enough to mount. Somebody better get that camera ready. It's getting close.

"Somebody get the gaff!" you shout, though unnecessarily. Somebody already has the gaff.

OK, keep the rod tip up and the slack out of the line. ... Come on fish, don't let go. ... Hooks don't fail me now.

The fish is almost to the boat. You feel it shaking its head, as if to say, "No, no, no, you're not going to catch me." Your heart races. A flash of the fish suddenly appears at the surface and vanishes just as quickly.

Whatever you do, don't knock it off with the gaff.

It's almost in...

And then the unthinkable. The unbelievable. The incomprehensible.

The line goes slack.

The electricity goes out in a finger snap, the adrenaline turning to molasses.

You are feeling empty as your worst fear is realized.

The catch of a lifetime dissolves into a memory, one that is shared by all fishermen. This great catch that wasn't meant to be has dreadfully become *THE ONE THAT GOT AWAY.*

In fishing, a worse feeling doesn't exist. It's like realizing you misread the lottery numbers after believing you hit the $40 million jackpot.

Tommy Resha of Birmingham, Alabama, knows the feeling better than most. The one that got away from him is the all-time heartbreaker, not only because of its size and what it was worth but for the length of time it fought before earning its freedom.

The blue marlin Resha hooked on April 20, 1999 would have meant $1.2 million for his team in the Bahamas Billfish Championship. The fish almost certainly would have beaten the Bahamian record of 1,060 pounds, if not the world record of 1,402 pounds.

In the end, however, only one record was set and a dubious one at that. It is the record for the longest fight by one angler on a fish that got away. Resha sat in the fighting chair aboard the *Abracadabra* battling that fish for 32 hours, 41 minutes.

"If I had thought I'd be there for 32 hours, 41 minutes, I'd have cut the line in the first five minutes," Resha says.

Ironically, as Resha traveled with captain Ronnie Riebe on the 46-foot Bertram from Florida to the Bahamas before the event, Riebe was reading a magazine that told of an angler who had fought a marlin for 30 hours in Kona, Hawaii.

When Riebe related the story, Resha shook his head. He couldn't imagine fighting a fish that long. Then he went out and fought one even longer, a feat he still finds unbelievable.

"I'll tell you what, you can't do anything for 32 hours and 41 minutes," he says. "If you had a hot tub full of starlets, you couldn't stay in with them that long."

Without any starlets on board to cheer him on, Resha hooked up to the fish of a lifetime at 11:20 on a Tuesday morning, the second day of the tournament.

The marlin hit a trolled jig and started racing out to sea, jumping several times. Resha took up his position in the fighting chair and held on. The reel got so hot so quickly, it burned to touch. Riebe was backing down on the fish as fast as the boat would go. Resha realized it wasn't fast enough when he looked at his reel.

"I could see the spool," he says. "I thought he was gone then. I thought he was going to take all the line and keep going."

But eventually the fish stopped and the team managed to regain most the line until, finally, the swivel at the end of the 15-foot wire leader hit the rod tip.

The only deckhand on board was Chris Mulcahy. The other returned home because of a family emergency. Mulcahy grabbed the leader and tried pulling in the fish. Once the blue felt this pressure, it was off to the races again.

This routine was repeated 67 times during the course of the battle.

"It's like holding a bull by the tail, trying to hold on to him," Resha says.

After five hours, captain Ron Schatman, a friend of Riebe who was also in the event, dropped off his two deckhands to help. At 4:30, it was lines out for other tournament boats not hooked up. The next day was a rest day so Schatman didn't need them again until Thursday, not that he thought they'd be out all day Wednesday.

So deckhands Emory Black and Sean Lang climbed aboard *Abracadabra*. Black couldn't wait to get a shot at the fish. He got his chance in the next hour. He grabbed hold of the leader. The fish wouldn't budge from its position 15 feet straight down behind the stern.

Black turned around and said, "It looks like a pilot whale. It's as big as an island."

He then turned to Resha and said, "You're gonna be here a long time."

"I've been here long enough," Resha replied.

But the fish had only begun to fight.

About one o'clock in the morning, on one of the 67 times they got the fish to leader, the fish got wrapped in the leader and was sideways. It sat there 50 or 60 feet behind the boat, not moving.

"All we could do was keep a tight line on him," Resha says. "He laid there in the water until 6 o'clock in the morning."

They waited so they could see enough to untangle the line. To pass the time and keep Resha in the game, the crew took turns telling jokes. Resha credits the comedy of Black for being the fuel that kept him going.

At dawn, they grabbed the leader and miraculously it untangled, and the fight resumed.

"He had more rest than I did," Resha recalls. "When it was time to go again, he was as green as he was when he first hit it. ... So now we're back at it again. Another run to hell and back. Of course, this time he only took maybe half the spool."

Back down on the fish, pull on the wire, watch the fish run. Back down on the fish, pull on the wire, watch the fish run. The routine became monotonous.

"All I heard was 'Wind, Tommy, wind; wind, Tommy, wind,'" Resha recalls. "I was crying like a baby in my heart."

He was probably also wishing he had never agreed to take over the fishing duties from his friend Ed Hardin, the boat's owner who was called away on business at the last moment.

"Don't worry about a thing captain, I got it," Resha would say, trying his best to reassure the crew he had it under control.

Privately he was thinking, "Please line, break. Please line, break."

In the heat and humidity of the tropics, Resha wore shorts, a t-shirt and sunglasses. He was barefoot. Black kept him lathered in sunscreen. Resha didn't eat but drank water almost nonstop and sweated profusely. He only peed once, early in the fight. He did that in his shorts. The crew washed him down with a bucket of water.

He couldn't very well get up and use the john. To hand the rod over to a crew member would mean disqualification. All that money would go down the drain. But this lottery ticket at the end of the line was proving tough to cash.

Riebe says every trick in the book they used was countered by the fish with a move of its own.

"He was playing me as much as I was playing him," Resha says. "I'll tell you this, he wasn't a rookie. That fish was not a rookie."

Neither was the team aboard *Abracadabra*. All were veteran big-game fishermen with countless years of experience. They fought the fish flawlessly and still the fish was winning.

Near the end, Riebe noticed the crew talking with Resha. A while later, a crew member climbed to the bridge to deliver this message: "Tommy's had it."

A deckhand held the wheel as Riebe went down to talk to Resha.

"This fish has whipped my butt," Resha said.

"Can you give me 10 more minutes?" Riebe asked.

"What good will that do?"

"I don't have any idea."

"Well, I'll give you 10 more minutes then I've gotta quit. I'm not going to make it."

Riebe called his crew to the bridge.

"I'm not going to kill this man for a dollar," he told them. "We've got to stop the fish and pop him. You guys get a hold of that leader and hang on for dear life."

On the 67th time the fish came to leader, two deckhands grabbed the 400-pound-test wire and pulled as mightily as possible.

Finally this game of chess was about to end. The fish, in its unwillingness to lose, finally reached the point of checkmate on Resha and his team.

At 8:01 Wednesday night, the leader snapped at the hook.

Resha was relieved. He had been thinking for the previous 15 hours that he couldn't go another minute but went much more. Yes, he was definitely relieved. It was over—finally!

The boat fell silent as Resha tried standing. He dropped to the deck, unable to walk. He crawled into the cabin and fell asleep on the floor.

Two deckhands retired to cabin bunks. Mulcahy climbed to the bridge to keep Riebe company for the four-hour ride back. They had chased the fish 35 miles from where it was hooked, leaving them nearly 50 miles from port.

Riebe couldn't help but think about Earnest Hemingway's award-winning book that was also a movie. He felt he had just lived through *The Old Man and the Sea.*

"In my 41 years, I've never seen anything like that," Riebe says.

To this day, he can still see that fish, as if it were in front of him. How big was it?

The back of the stern measured 14 feet, 10 inches. As they looked at the fish 15 feet below the surface, they could see it extended well beyond both ends of the stern. The fish was 17, 18 or 19 feet long. The Bahamian record blue went 14 feet.

"I said the fish was between 1,200 and 1,500 pounds, but the fish had a lot of girth at the tail and the shoulders," Riebe says. "The fish was really heavy, so I think 1,500 pounds is a pretty close guess."

As the *Abracadabra* backed into its slip at the dock just before midnight, the two dozen people who had waited for the boat to return gave them a rousing ovation, as they would later at the awards banquet.

"It gave me chills," Riebe says.

The team did not fish Thursday, Day 3 of the tournament. Instead, it took a much-needed day of rest. Heaven knows Resha needed it.

"The next day, the hair on my head was sore," Resha relates. "Every part of my body was sore from one end to the other. My toes were sore. He kicked my fat butt and I'm not kidding you. That fish definitely kicked my butt.

"He was a magnificent creature. He deserved to get away. It would've been a shame to kill that fish looking back in retrospect."

Resha called the fish "the ultimate one that got away" and who can argue?

After recharging its batteries, the team was ready to try again Friday, the last day of the tournament. As the *Abracadabra* motored out to the marlin grounds, one thought kept popping into Resha's mind:

"I hope to God the same one doesn't hit again."

GENERAL H. NORMAN SCHWARZKOPF

A walking cast acted like an anchor as General H. Norman Schwarzkopf fished the shoreline of an Alaskan lake near Resurrection Bay. Like a Las Vegas gambler glued to his seat in front of a hot slot machine, the general hit jackpot after jackpot.

Using a green lure he purchased from a discount tackle store, "where you get 10,000 lures for five bucks," Schwarzkopf was nailing Dolly Varden after Dolly Varden.

General Norman Schwarzkopf poses with a seven-pound, two-ounce Dolly Vardon trout he landed in Alaska. It was once a world record for two-pound-test line. An unidentified guide holds the fish for the general.
Photo courtesy of General Norman Schwarzkopf

When his wife arrived, he couldn't wait to show her how his magical lure worked.

"I've got this incredible lure, you should see this, Brenda," he told his wife. "Every time I throw it in I catch a fish."

The magic continued until Schwarzkopf suddenly hooked into a large fish, one he dearly wanted to land, a fish of a lifetime. But then the unthinkable occurred.

"The fish wraps itself around a snag right in front of me in the water," says Schwarzkopf, who was helpless because of the cast from Achilles' tendon surgery.

"So I turned to my wife and said, 'If you reeeeeally love me.' My poor wife, in a pair of blue jeans, is wading out into this ice-cold water to pull this snag loose. I said, 'Whatever you do, don't touch the line, don't touch the line.'

"Well, as luck would have it, she started to slip and immediately reached out and grabbed the line and, of course, broke the fish off. But the worst part was, this fish was swimming away with my lure in its mouth—the magic lure."

As the fish swam off, it became bigger and bigger, and the playful scolding began.

"'Obviously, I just lost the world-record Dolly Varden because you did this'—I was kidding her," Schwarzkopf says. "Of course, she's soaking wet from all the water, but I'm not paying attention. I'm looking at my lure swimming off."

Years later, Schwarzkopf returned to Alaska and caught a seven-pound, two-ounce Dolly Varden, his fish of a lifetime. But the one that got away is remembered most in the household, particularly by Mrs. Schwarzkopf.

"She's never really forgiven me for that," Schwarzkopf says, smiling.

CURT GOWDY

Revered and renowned sports broadcaster Curt Gowdy was behind the microphone for practically every sporting event known to man, yet people remember him most as the host of the original *American Sportsman*.

For 20 years, Gowdy brought celebrities and the outdoors into the living rooms of millions of TV viewers every Sunday afternoon on ABC. The fishing and hunting outdoors show was unrivaled and it earned Gowdy six Emmy Awards as host and co-producer.

Bing Crosby and Phil Harris, seasoned outdoorsmen, helped produce several memorable episodes with a cast from a fishing rod, a blast from a shotgun and several catchy tunes from their vocal cords.

Nevertheless, the highlight from all those years on the air was created by a quarterback from the Pittsburgh Steelers. It was Terry Bradshaw stealing the show of all-time shows.

The episode aired in the mid- to late 1970s when the Steelers were Super Bowl kings. The location was Key West, Florida. The target was big tarpon.

The best method of catching tarpon is with a fly rod and streamer, but that presented a problem. Bradshaw didn't know how to use a fly

Curt Gowdy on a river in New Zealand.
Photo courtesy of Curt Gowdy

rod. Oh, he could cast a spinning rod as easily as he could complete a pass to Lynn Swan.

So that's what he used. For two days, he tossed a variety of lures using a spinning rod. This produced nary a bite. Nada, zilch, nothing. The tarpon turned their noses at everything in the tackle box.

Finally, the guide informed Gowdy that if they were to save the show and catch a tarpon, Bradshaw would have to learn how use a fly rod and streamer.

The audible was called and Bradshaw eagerly accepted lessons on this new fishing method. After two hours of practice, he was ready to give it a try.

The next day, they anchored the boat in four or five feet of water. Over the ocean floor of white sand, big tarpon could easily be seen swimming.

Gowdy gave some last-minute instructions.

"If this fish takes, Terry, probably the first thing it's going to do is jump," Gowdy explained. "When he goes up in the air, you bow your rod so there's no tension on the leader because he'll come down and crash and break it. As soon as he's in the water, set the hook again.

"If he starts to run, you've got some loose line here on the deck, let it go through the guides smoothly. What I do is form an 'O' with my finger. The line runs through it so it doesn't get caught around my hand or fingers or anything like that."

Bradshaw understood but insisted upon Gowdy going first. The host, a fly fisher his entire life, hooked and landed an 80-pounder. Now it was Bradshaw's turn.

Bradshaw started casting. The first tarpon making a pass wouldn't take the fly. On the second, Bradshaw pulled the fly out of its mouth. On the third, he connected, setting the hook on a big tarpon.

"It corkscrewed right up into the air," Gowdy recalled. "We yelled, 'Bow, bow, bow the rod.' He bowed the rod. He did fine there. He came back and set the hook again and the fish took off.

"But Terry forgot about the smooth entrance into the guides and he got his fingers all tangled around his line and the tarpon took that rod and yanked it right out of his hands and out over the water.

"Terry backed up and did a swan dive into the water and was swimming after the fish and the rod. I never laughed so hard in my life. It's the only time I ever saw a fish catch a man."

Curt Gowdy with outdoors writer Homer Circle,
who is weighing a largemouth bass.
Photo courtesy of Curt Gowdy

Fortunately for Gowdy, Bradshaw managed to retrieve the rod and reel, the fly having worked itself free from the fish's mouth.

"I had a $350 reel on that rod so I was glad to get it back," Gowdy says. "He called out from the water and started laughing himself. He was a good sport about it, but boy did we give it to him. Finally, he got a tarpon on and landed it, and he was thrilled."

Bradshaw wasn't nearly as excited to see the clip of his dive into the water played over and over on a couple of talk shows, though.

"He called me up one time and said, 'Geez, don't show that again, it makes me look so stupid,'" Gowdy says. "I said, 'Aw, no it doesn't. It's one of the greatest fishing shows we've ever had.'"

BILL ENGVALL

One time while fishing the Blanco River in Texas, Bill Engvall got a bass, catfish, some perch and quite a scare as he prepared to leave for home.

"It was getting to be about dusk and so I started breaking down the pole and stuff," the comedian says. "I reached down and grabbed my stringer and lifted it up and took three steps and realized there was a water moccasin hanging on the end fish. I went, 'Jeez!!!' I threw the whole stringer and fish back into the water.

"It was a buffet for the snakes that day."

KEN GRIFFEY JR.

If you're scoring at home, give Ken Griffey Jr. a throwing error, but don't be too hard on him. He was only 14 years old at the time.

Ken Griffey Sr. purchased three brand-new fishing rods totaling in the neighborhood of $550 and took his son fishing off a pier in Fort Lauderdale. The target was bluefish.

After a couple of casts, it happened.

"I went to cast and threw the whole thing into the water," Griffey Jr. recalls. "My dad looked at me and just started laughing because I guess he'd done it before."

After five minutes of attempting to retrieve the outfit, the pair went back to the car and got the other rod.

"It was something funny," Griffey Jr. says.

Years later, after Griffey Jr. had become a star center fielder with the Seattle Mariners, he went bass fishing with outdoors TV star Jimmy Houston in Texas and enjoyed his most memorable fishing outing.

"Every other cast we were catching something," Griffey Jr. says. "Even then, I almost lost my rod and reel, nearly throwing it into the water. I'm left-handed, but I cast right-handed. It feels funny. It's awkward."

This time, however, he managed to catch the rod before it got away.

"Next time," he promised, "I'm going to wear my batting glove and stick 'um."

TRACY BYRD

The cow paddy hit the fan when Tracy Byrd lost a big largemouth bass at the boat while fishing with his father over a flooded cow pasture on Sam Rayburn Lake in Texas in the late 1980s.

The country music star, an avid angler, had hooked a six-pound bass using a spinnerbait. By any standard, it was an impressive fish, only Byrd fumbled it.

"I fought her for a few seconds there and got her up to the side of the boat and instead of lipping her or netting her, I just thought I'd swing her in because she was headed toward the boat anyway," Byrd said.

Big mistake. As he pulled the fish out of the water, the line broke at the knot, and the fish and his lure were lost. Since Byrd's father Jerry enjoys teasing his son whenever he loses a big fish, the lost bass brought on the barbs.

"Well, that one smoked you, didn't it?" Jerry said. "You couldn't handle it. Just like I say, you can't handle the big ones."

A couple hours later, Byrd returned to the flooded cow pasture.

"Around the same spot I hooked the big bass, I got a bump on the worm, set the hook and fought the fish," Byrd recalled. "It was another good fish and I reeled her up and started to reach down to lip her and there was my spinnerbait hanging out of her mouth. It was the same fish."

Byrd removed the spinnerbait and the worm, and released the fish, having become the rare angler who caught the one that got away.

"I had the last laugh on my old man that day," Byrd said.

Country star Tracy Byrd poses with a largemouth bass.
Photo courtesy of Star Keeper Public Relations

Chapter Eleven

The Joke-Stars

The fishing was slow and the reality show was in need of reel humor. Ozzy Osbourne, the garbage-mouthed rock star, was filming an installment of *The Osbournes* for MTV aboard the New Del Mar sportfishing boat out of Marina del Rey, California.

In this episode, Ozzy was had by one of the most common practical jokes in fishing: The old pretend-there's-a-fish-at-the-end-of-the-line trick used with a bucket or soda cans filled with water.

Osbourne was fishing with his son, Jack, and brother-in-law when the brother-in-law took skipper Ricky Carbajal aside and asked him to do something funny. Carbajal was happy to oblige.

He filled three soda cans with water, tied them to a line, lowered them into the water and let it sink a spell. Then he raised the rod to "set the hook" and handed the rod to Ozzy.

If the current is strong, the cans or bucket can actually act like a big fish pulling at the end of the line and that's what it was doing with Ozzy, who probably thought he hooked a marlin.

"He was saying it was [bleeping] heavy and [bleeping] fighting hard and everybody was cheering him," Carbajal recalls.

When Osbourne finally got his "catch" to the surface, he was out for blood after realizing he'd been duped.

"He grabbed a fillet knife and was saying, 'I'm going to kill you!'" Carbajal remembers.

The cast and crew could hardly contain themselves over this "canned" humor.

Over the years, anglers have concocted innumerable variations of this trick and I've come across plenty of them, many from members of Allcoast Sportfishing and Coastside Fishing Club. Check these out:

A guy with a hangover fell asleep. His buddies tied a five-gallon bucket to his salmon line and tossed it behind the boat and let it out 200 yards. They turned the clicker on and when the reel started going off— zzzzzz—they started yelling, "You've got one!" It took him 30 minutes to pull in the bucket and, like Osbourne, he was ready to kill when he saw he'd been duped.

Imagine the surprised look on the faces of anglers who reeled in the carcass of a filleted halibut, a filleted dorado, a bucket with a bowling ball, a frozen five-pound channel catfish, a frozen chicken, a rubber chicken with weights in it and a sheep's head—not the fish called sheepshead but the actual head of a sheep!

Playing a practical joke while fishing is sometimes needed to help break the tedium of waiting for fish to bite. They create laughs and memories that are often relived into old age.

The bucket tied to the end of the line is one of many. Another favorite is stealthily pulling on the fishing line and making the rod tip bend as if a fish were tugging, making the victim believe a fish really was tugging.

On the overnight charter boats, best be careful lest you be the brunt of a practical joke. The multi-day boats especially see a share of them.

Anglers sleeping in their bunks wake up in the morning to the sounds of "Hook up, hook up!" As they reach for their boots, they find they have been filled with water and frozen while they slept. This trick sometimes includes a mackerel in each boot.

Looking for an amusing alarm clock? Put a live mackerel into a plastic grocery bag and toss it into the bunk of a sleeping angler. This'll create plenty of laughs for everyone—everyone but the sleeping angler.

Anchovies and sardines seem to show up in all kinds of places besides on a hook ready to be cast. They are put down the back of pants, into boots, into cans of beer and into tackle boxes at the end of trips, only to be discovered a few days later smelling up the garage.

Squid ink has a place on the practical joke list. It is smeared on the outer edges of binoculars. Black rings are left around the eyes of the unsuspecting.

Keep a close eye on your gear. You never know what a prankster might do. Anglers find their reels put on their rods backwards or cast without knowing the cast control knob is wide open, causing the mother of all bird's nests. They find their tackle box Super Glued shut or find a seagull in their tackle bags.

Funny, too, is when the victim refuses to fall for the same trick, even when it's not a trick. *You got me once on the old bucket at the end of the line spoof, I ain't gonna fall for that one again.* Only when the fish jumps on the horizon are they convinced a real fish is on the line.

Sometimes a joke is not worth playing. Sometimes it can come back to haunt you. Like the teenager who made a post on a popular fishing Website in Southern California, telling everyone he had caught an albacore in Newport Harbor. He even posted a photo. It caused quite a stir. Was he telling the truth? After all, the chances of his catching an albacore in the harbor were about equal to his catching one in a freshwater lake.

After a while, he admitted it was a joke gone bad.

About a year later, word hit the fishing community that the same teenager had caught a 35-pound yellowtail from the Balboa Pier, a story just as unbelievable as the albacore in the harbor. Was he telling the truth?

Nobody believed him. He became the boy who cried wolf because as it turned out, it was true. The story was confirmed by reputable witnesses who were there the day he caught it. A hard lesson was learned.

Philip Friedman once pulled what was literally a "practical" joke since it helped his 976-tuna.com charter catch more yellowtail than the rest of the sportfishing fleet.

Like all the other boats, they were chasing bird schools at San Clemente Island off Southern California. Birds would start working an area, diving into the water for an easy meal. They were feeding on the baitfish pushed up by schools of yellowtail. Anglers would see the birds and race over to catch yellowtail. As many as 10 boats made the mad dash to get on the fish.

"If you weren't the first boat throwing some iron or bait, you didn't get a fish," Friedman explains.

So when Friedman spotted some yellowtail surfacing off the bow, he chummed off the stern with his over-stocked supply of donuts and raced over to the spot of yellowtail.

"The birds got all over the donuts," he says. "Then 10 sportboats would run to the donuts and we'd have the yellows to ourselves. We'd get the first shot at those schools by doing that."

The prank sounds like something out of the fishing joke book of the Los Pescadores, a Southern California fishing club that lives for the practical joke during its annual Los Pescadores Billfish Tournament. The tourney was created in 1990 as a means of making fun of local, no-nonsense, way-too-serious marlin tournaments.

The "Peskys" event was designed to be 100 percent fun and nonsense. For instance, teams are awarded bonus points for a photo of the angler and the bagel adorning the bill of the striped marlin he caught. This is the Peskys' version of tagging and releasing. Also, entrants are warned, "fishing too seriously is grounds for disqualification."

The joke of all practical jokes was pulled during this tournament in the mid 1990s. Matt Earl of the organizing committee came up with the idea of making fake marlin tails and spreading them out all over the ocean.

With a painted cutout resembling a marlin tail connected to 1.5-inch PVC pipe, these phonies would float on top of the surface and get the adrenaline flowing in those anglers who came upon them.

"It looks like a real fish," said Andy Crean, who helped create the tails. "The calmer the water the better they look. If you come up on one and look at it, it looks identical. You can't tell unless you study it and see how it floats."

They made 100 of them. Without telling anyone, they motored out from tournament headquarters on Catalina Island hours before the start of the event and began planting the jokes.

Zigzagging toward a bank where the marlin were supposed to be, they dropped a fake tail every so often until all the floating funnies were in position.

"So everybody gets up and drives east looking for tailers and start coming across them," Crean explains. "Then the word gets out over the radio that there are these fake ones. The problem is, there are also a lot of real ones. So everybody would have to drive up to one when they'd see them in the binoculars to find out if they were real or fake."

On some, they would hook a mackerel to the end of an eight-foot leader and attach it to the fake tail. The swimming mackerel made the tail change directions, giving it life.

Sometimes they would leave a fake tale and add a calling card: A paper plate full of potato chips. The birds descended upon the chips, creating the effect of a feeding frenzy that drew the attention of anglers.

Plenty of fake tails were baited before anglers realized they'd been had. Funny, the prank worked so well, it even got the pranksters.

Late in the afternoon, the *Bounder*, the boat with Earl, Crean & Jokesters Unlimited, came upon a sleeping marlin or what they thought was a real sleeping marlin.

After looking at it from the bow, Randy Wood turned around. He wasn't about to toss a live mackerel to a phony tail.

"I can tell a fake one when I see one," he replied. "You're not going to get me on that. I know you're messing with me."

About that time, the marlin tail swam away, and the billfish it belonged to never was tempted to take the bait because the bait was never tossed its way.

"Tailgate" was worth countless laughs. Yet not everybody found it funny, especially the anglers participating in a big-money marlin tournament held two days later.

"They didn't see as much humor in it," Crean said.

Wasting time baiting a fake tail when thousands of dollars are at stake is not funny to the serious tournament angler.

Of course, the Los Pescadores loved it: A practical joke without an expiration date.

The fishing world has all kinds of comedic characters, some who enjoy a practical joke, others who merely enjoy clowning around. There's nothing quite like having a jokester around to tickle the funny bone when you're fishing.

JOHNNY MILLER

Water hazards on a golf course can produce not only great fishing but great adventure, as former professional golfer Johnny Miller often found.

Many a day he would finish a round of golf and replace his clubs with a fishing rod and head back onto the course when all was clear. He never knew what he'd catch next. Or what he'd try to catch.

On the fifth hole of the old Sawgrass Course at TPC in Jacksonville, Florida, Miller noticed a nine-foot alligator on the other side of a small lake.

"I decided to throw my plastic worm over in front of him," he says. "I thought it would be sort of interesting. He grabbed at it but missed. I threw it back again and he grabbed at it and missed again. But he jumped into the water. So I reeled it back across the water, as fast as I could. I was looking all over for this alligator because now I'm thinking about maybe trying to catch him in the water. I looked down and this alligator was ONE FOOT from me. He had swum as fast as my worm was being reeled in and with no wake at all.

"He could have just grabbed me and pulled me down. My eyes got very large. I slowly backed up and had to go home and change my shorts."

Another time, on a golf course at Hilton Head, South Carolina, Miller actually succeeded in catching an alligator—a three-footer—by accident.

Wanting to show the kids, the jokester put it in a tennis bag and took it back to the hotel, putting it into the bathtub.

"The worst part about it was, I had him in there about three hours and I forgot to tell the maid and when she went in to clean the room, there was this loud scream," Miller says. "That's a true story. The alligator was cool. It didn't hurt him. I put him back afterward."

Miller did not follow the same catch-and-release philosophy on another exotic catch he made at Hilton Head, however.

After snagging a turtle in the foot, he decided to take it home and release it into the lake on his Napa, California property.

"I put it in my handbag at the airport," he recalls. "It went through the X-ray machine and showed a little bit dark, I guess. The lady stuck her hand in there to see what it was and it bit her. I thought I was going to go to jail for illegally transporting wildlife across state lines."

Turns out, the lady inspector was disliked by her co-workers, who thought it was the greatest thing they'd ever seen.

"That turtle is still at my lake and doing just fine," Miller says.

But please don't tell the local game warden.

CLAY WALKER

Country music star Clay Walker considers his father-in-law a great friend. They often fish together, usually catching all the red fish they want off the jetties near Walker's hometown of Beaumont, Texas.

One trip started out unlike any other. His father-in-law wanted to make a wager and Walker agreed.

"We went and had a little $5 bet that he would catch the first fish," Walker says. "Well, he handed me a pole and I put mine in the water and he put his in the water. Next thing you know, he pulls up a fish. So I lost the bet.

"I'm still doodle-socking the bait—that's bouncing the bait up and down on the floor of the rocks—and he catches another fish. I said, 'I can't believe this. OK, triple or nothing.'

"He said, 'Man, you might want to check that bait to make sure those hooks aren't tangled up.' I said, 'My hooks aren't tangled up, I'd be able to tell it.' He said, 'No, check that bait.' I pulled it up and it didn't have any hooks. He took the hooks off my lure.

"Needless to say, I didn't pay."

TOM DREESEN

While growing up on the south side of Chicago, Tom Dreesen went fishing with his buddies once in a while but never developed the feel for it.

But as a stand-up comedian who toured for more than a decade with Frank Sinatra and who appeared on *The Tonight Show* more than 60 times, Dreesen knows the value of a good fish story.

"There was an old guy down in Alabama. When I ran away from home as a kid, I went throughout Alabama. This old guy right outside Huntsville told me that he went fishing every Saturday in a creek down the way that has fish in it so big you have to tie your line to a mule to pull them out.

"So I went over there on a Saturday morning and I saw him down there, and he was fishing and I said to him, 'I don't see your mule.' He said, 'Last fish pulled him dead into the river.'"

ROGER CLEMENS

Baseball great Roger Clemens only thought he was going fishing close to home. Instead, friends took him for a ride. A long ride.

"I think that's the way they lured me out of the house," Clemens said. "I thought I was going to fish about 45 minutes from the house, possibly Lake Conrow out of Houston. I had a day to mess around. I thought we were going for a short fishing trip. No problem, fish half a day and get back home.

"When I woke up in the car and we were still not there and they said only a few more miles, it was another three hours. I think we ended up 15 minutes outside of Dallas or somewhere. We were at Lake Fork. It ended up being a four-and-a-half-hour road trip. And I froze. It was sleeting and raining, and I think I got one nibble on one of those bass in Lake Fork."

The one thing he learned from the experience: Patience.

"Like anything, you have to put your time into it before you get rewarded."

Presumably he meant time on the water, not on the road.

CLINT BLACK

Fishing never became a big part of Clint Black's life, contrary to what his bio leads you to believe. He did *not* serve as a fishing guide to make ends meet before becoming a country singing star.

"That was something my first manager made up and I could never get rid of," Black said.

The little fishing Black *has* done since hitting the big time is deep sea.

"I've spent over 30 hours out in the deep waters around the Hawaiian Islands and I caught a skipjack tuna and that's it. That's a sad fishing story."

Obviously it wasn't a catch he was too proud of, considering the fish-rich waters of Hawaii.

"I didn't mount the skipjack," he dead-panned.

GARY McCORD

Golfer Gary McCord was fishing with a buddy, Ed Campbell, in Vail, Colorado, when he was forced to improvise to win a bet.

"We go out fishing and we don't know what we're doing, but we got all this stuff. We're in the Eagle River and it's five dollars for the first fish.

"Basically, we just try not to fall in the water. But we got all this fly-fishing stuff. We're doing dry flies and we're out there with our waders and we're doing the deal. We can't fish. No way we can catch any.

"So my buddy, Ed, is down the river a little bit and I see this dead fish floating by. Ed's up there so I kind of sneak over, pick it up and hook it up. I threw him over here and, 'Oh, look at this!' I'm bouncing the thing up and down in the water. 'Look, look at this fish going.'

"I got my five dollars and never told him."

ELGIN BAYLOR

When it relates to fishing bait, an anchovy is an anchovy, unless former NBA great Elgin Baylor is telling a tall tale, in which case beware: Don't get caught swallowing the yarn hook, line and sinker.

Baylor's friend, Bob, did.

They were fishing aboard a crowded sportfishing boat near Anacapa Island off Oxnard, California, in the late 1980s when the yellowtail were running strong.

Though Bob is a veteran saltwater angler, albeit a gullible one, he was having a hard time keeping up with Baylor as the NBA Hall of

Famer caught fish after fish, despite having never caught a yellowtail before.

Everybody else was catching fish, but Bob, who tried everything. Baylor even changed spots and fishing rods with Bob. Still Bob couldn't catch a fish.

"In the end, I caught a whole bunch of yellowtail and he got nothing, and I think his wife caught one," Baylor remembers.

Later, at a friend's house, they got to talking about the trip and Bob started in about Baylor being the luckiest guy in the world, catching all those fish.

"Wait a minute," Baylor said. "It wasn't luck. It was skill."

"What are you talking about, you don't even know how to fish." Bob replied.

"What were you using for bait?" Baylor asked.

"The same thing you were using—anchovies," Bob replied.
"But were you using male or female? I was using female anchovies."

"What do you mean male or female? That's a bunch of bull. How are you going to tell them apart?"

"Easy, the female is much lighter underneath than the male. The male is darker."

Baylor assumed Bob dismissed it as the joke that it was, but a week later found out otherwise when Bob went fishing with his wife, again for yellowtail.

"When the boat stopped at the bait barge to get bait, Bob went up to the captain and told him, 'You better make sure you get plenty of female anchovies,'" Baylor relates.

"I swear. His wife told us the story. She said you should have seen the skipper's face. The guy just looked at him. The guy thought he was nuts.

"I went by Bob's office and told him his wife had told me what happened. He admitted to it. He said, 'Don't you tell anybody.' I said, 'If I do, I won't use your name.'

"Every time I see him, he starts laughing. I remind him of it— female anchovies!"

Chapter Twelve

Family Ties

Fishing is more than the tug at the end of the line, a monster fish peeling line off the reel, a red-and-white bobber pulled below the surface, a fish squirming in the net, a friend clicking off a photo of you and your catch.

Fishing is more than fresh air, sunshine, leaves turning colors, wind whispering through the trees, a bald eagle perched on a tree top, a hawk gliding on a rising thermal, a beaver swimming up river, an elk drinking from a stream.

Fishing is more than basking in the beauty of a creek, stream, river, farm pond, lake or ocean. It's more than a tent, campfire and fish tacos. More than enjoying the peaceful environs that are far removed from rush-hour traffic, ringing telephones and blaring televisions.

Fishing is also family. It means sharing quality time with son and daughter, mother and father, husband and wife, grandfather and grandmother, grandson and granddaughter. Grab a rod and reel, pull up a dock, open a carton of worms and dabble in the world of family bonding.

"When you get out on the water with a son, daughter, mother, father or grandfather and grandmother, nothing is in the way. No telephone, no dinner table, it's just you and them," says Bruce Matthews, president and CEO of the Recreational Boating and Fishing Foundation. "It's the best time to talk about stuff. Stuff that really means something. It's more than about catching fish.

"To me, it's all about the stories. It's the stories you build on the water that you tell over and over.

"Fish stories are kind of the glue in a lot of ways that cement family relationships together. The opportunities to build those stories are unparalleled in a fishing and boating context."

The first step toward constructing a story is laying a fishing foundation. Gordon Holland, who promotes fishing as a "wonderful family activity," has introduced thousands of youngsters to fishing with his Hooked on Fishing International organization and its many annual fishing derbies.

"It's just a matter of getting mom or dad or the family to take a youngster out fishing for the first time," Holland says. "Get a camera because it's going to be a memory forever. It gives the parents something to do with their children, that they can collectively enjoy and then continue to grow with as the child gets older."

Unlike skateboarding, rock climbing or mountain biking, fishing is something families can enjoy together for the rest of their lives. For some, fishing can even save lives.

Putting a rod and reel in the hands of a youngster can be like handing them a divining rod for the future. It steers them away from trouble.

"There's so many directions that are available to a child nowadays, most of them good, thank goodness, and a few bad," Holland says. "This is a sport that we very adamantly believe will keep them on the right path.

"I've never seen a youngster who really likes to fish go bad. I've just never heard of it."

President Herbert Hoover once said, "No one commits crime while fishing."

Introduce fishing to children before they turn 14 and chances are excellent they'll continue the sport into adulthood. In some families, giving a child that first fishing rod represents a rite of passage of sorts, the torch being handed down from one generation to the next.

The Bush Family is a wonderful example of family and fishing, and the angling tradition blossoming on the family tree.

President George Bush's exploits with a fishing rod are well documented. Salmon, trout, bass, dorado, tarpon, kings and bluefish are among the species he has targeted. It's no secret fishing is his favorite pastime, his favorite activity for relaxation.

President George W. Bush has the same passion in his blood. He stocked largemouth bass in a pond on his ranch in Crawford, Texas. It's his own personal getaway. And as his father did, George W. passed the sport down to his daughters.

In August 2004, the son of Jeb Bush was getting married in Kennebunkport, Maine. George W. used the opportunity to take his father and twin daughters fishing on his father's new boat. Jenna landed a 38-inch striped bass.

As news organizations in other boats watched and took photos, George W., acting as the proud father, shouted out, "Get that fish? Thirty-eight inches. Jenna caught it!"

"It's an example of the first family being the first fishing family," said Mike Nussman, president of the American Sportfishing Association. "They spent a nice day together. Do they do it all the time? No. But is it something they all enjoy and do when they have the opportunity? Yes. They set a great example for all Americans."

The Future Fisherman Foundation, an offshoot from Nussman's association, attempts to set a different sort of example with its Hooked on Fishing—Not on Drugs educational program.

The mentor-based program used in more than 30 states not only teaches kids how to fish but helps them make positive life choices and educates them on caring for the environment. What an awesome message to be spreading among today's youth.

Just plain ol' fishing is the simple but poignant message delivered by the Recreational Boating and Fishing Foundation. A series of "Take me fishing" ads give emotional pleas that make it hard to say no.

"Take me fishing," a little girl says, "because my wedding will be sooner than you think."

"Take me fishing," a boy says, "because our boat is cooler than any video game."

"Take me fishing," a woman says, "and make me feel 16 again."

"Take me fishing," an elderly man pleads, "because I miss my boy."

"Take me fishing," a boy says, "so we'll always have something in common."

A grandfather baits the hook for his grandson. He helps the boy cast. After a while, the bobber dips below the surface. The boy reels in a nice trout. Their faces light up—a flashbulb illuminating a memory that will last a lifetime.

A son and his parents troll Alaskan waters for salmon. Even in rough conditions, they catch salmon after salmon. It's a trip of a lifetime.

A daughter and her parents share a boat on a mountain lake. They breath in the fresh air, take note of the deer along the shoreline, watch as an eagle soars overhead and share stories about school, work and play. They don't catch a thing but vow to return sometime soon with their rods and reels.

"The fishing part of it is not all that important as far as keeping a load of fish," Holland says. "It's just the fun of being out there and the ability to communicate with somebody else and communicate with nature."

Take the family fishing. Start building memories.

BOBBY KNIGHT

The fly-fishing trip to Wyoming was only four days away when famed broadcaster Curt Gowdy phoned Coach Bobby Knight to tell him he had to cancel because of a family emergency. This left Knight scrambling to find another fishing partner.

Like a high school senior trying to find a date for the prom at the last minute, Knight got on the phone and started making calls while his wife Karen sat reading a book.

"I call three people to see who might go with me and nobody can," Knight says. "I'm leaving in three or four days and nobody can go. So after the third person, I start looking at Karen and every time I look at her, I call somebody else.

Bobby Knight with wife Karen on a fishing trip to Colorado.
Karen has become an accomplished fly fisher.
Photo courtesy of Bobby Knight

"Finally, after six people I turn to her and I say, 'Hey, how would you like to go fishing with me in Wyoming on Friday?' She looked at me and said, 'You know, I think I'd really like that and I can't tell you how much it means to me that I'm the first person you asked.'"

Yes, well...

Karen wasn't the first choice largely because she had never fished before. But since she's a good athlete, Knight figured she could learn this sport that he is so enamored with.

"So I taught her the rudiments of casting, and she was not bad," Knight says. "She was actually going to be OK. Obviously, the creek was a little different than the backyard and so she fell in twice in the first 30 minutes.

"The second time she got up, she had on a felt hat and water was just dripping from it like a sprinkler, off every corner, and I was sitting on a rock kind of wondering how the hell I got into this. She looked over at me and—it was great—she said, 'You know, it's hard to play at your best when the coach is on your ass all the time.'"

Knight readily agreed. Since then, Karen has become an accomplished fly fisher and has fished all over with her husband, enjoying not only catching fish but being outdoors. Reading a book under a tree might be part of her fishing experience. So she doesn't always fish 100 percent of the time.

On one trip, Karen landed a nine-pound rainbow trout. As the guide released the fish after taking a photo, Karen started putting her rod away and Knight asked why.

"How can I get any better than that?" she replied.

ANDY GARCIA

While fishing offshore in the Bahamas, actor Andy Garcia survived a sudden electrical storm that made his hair stand at attention like Don King's.

Driving rain and darkness enveloped the boat that could have become a coffin for Garcia and some family members if not for the local knowledge of their skipper, Burke Rolle, who got them back safely.

On Bimini Island, native islanders grow up in and on the water, learning its tendencies like a fish. Burke Rolle was cut from this mold.

Garcia came to know Burke during frequent vacations to Bimini Island, the western-most island in the Bahamas known for its premier fishing and diving, and being the possible site of the lost continent of Atlantis.

The Garcia family stayed at the Bimini Bay Guest House run by Basil and Antoinette Rolle. Burke was their son. He was Garcia's fishing and diving guide.

"We got to know him very well because we'd see him all the time and he became sort of an extended member of our family every time we went to Bimini," Garcia says.

Burke used to dazzle Garcia with an awesome display of swimming and underwater marksmanship.

"We'd free dive for lobster and go probably 30 feet at most," Garcia recalls. "Time and time again I'd see him chase down lobsters as they propelled themselves with that jerky movement. I was always amazed by the way this kid moved in the water."

Another time, they went spearfishing with Hawaiian slings. A spear goes through a hole in the middle of a wooden handle and you pull back to load, then let go to fire.

"It's an underwater slingshot," Garcia explains. "This is the way you have to spearfish in the Bahamas because the other guns are illegal.

"So we're diving in 30 or 40 feet of water off north Bimini and my brother-in-law was maybe 50 yards away with his son. He pops his head out of the water and says, 'There's a school of mackerel coming your way.'"

Spanish mackerel are two to three feet long, six inches wide and move through the water as quickly as a sleek sports car. In other words, not an easy target.

Garcia and Burke took deep breaths and descended into the water column where the school of 10 to 20 mackerel would be swimming. When Burke saw the direction the school was headed, he ignited the afterburners and left Garcia behind to position himself for a shot.

"I became an observer because there's no way I'm going to get a Hawaiian sling shot at a Spanish mackerel," Garcia recalls. "That's like a William Tell-type of shot. It's just an impossibility."

Being as stealthy as possible, Burke approached the school until he was within range.

"As he was propelling himself forward, he reeled back and pulled that Hawaiian sling and shot, and hit a Spanish mackerel right behind the gill, which is the exact spot you want to hit a fish," Garcia says.

"He struck one of these fish in midwater as it was traveling. I've never seen anything like it in my life. He went and grabbed it and came out of the water with a big smile.

"I said to him, 'That's the most extraordinary thing I've ever seen in my life.' He just kind of smiled, as if to say, 'It's no big deal,' like it was just part of the local sport."

A talented athlete, a strong individual, a big set of pearly whites—Burke is someone Garcia will always remember, and never quite understand.

Why did Burke try to make the 50-mile crossing to Miami at night when native instincts said it was unwise? Why didn't he listen to the concerns of his parents?

"The great irony is, he died young—probably in his early 30s," Garcia says. "He was lost at sea. The parents urged him not to go that night, and he never returned."

Conditions the night Burke was lost were far more predictable than the day Burke helped Garcia and family survive. That storm came as suddenly as a lightning bolt.

They were fishing a reef called the Great Isaacs, making impressive catches of yellowtail snapper, grouper and other bottom fish. This was in the 1980s, the pre-electronics era, so Burke navigated by compass and monitored the weather by sight.

The area is notorious for its sudden summer squalls.

"It just creeps up on you," Garcia says. "You're fishing and the weather is fine, then all of a sudden you look up and go, 'Hey, look at the cloud that's coming.' Then you realize that cloud is between you and Bimini.

"You can't go away because you could run out of gas. You can't just sit there. So it becomes one of those hairy situations where you know you're going to get hit because it's coming right at you and you cannot outrun it."

Burke had no choice but to fire up the engine and head into the coming storm. "Let's go," he told the group.

The anglers were exposed in Burke's open, 24-foot boat with no cabin to seek refuge. Soon, the skies darkened, lightning cracked, thunder clapped, rain pelted the anglers in sheets, the temperature dropped more than 30 degrees and visibility became nil.

Burke opened the throttle as much as he dared and the anglers held on for dear life. They worried, however, about holding on to the aluminum t-top that surrounded the steering column, fearing a lightning strike would light them up.

Electricity was in the air.

"Literally, your hair stands straight up like you see characters in cartoons," Garcia says.

Garcia maintained faith in the man he grew to respect, yet the experience was still a little frightening.

"They know their way around," Garcia says. "They've been in that kind of situation. It's like their backyard so that kind of weather condition is constantly around them. It doesn't intimidate them as much as it does us. But he wasn't messing around. He wasn't whistling Dixie or anything, but he knew what he was doing.

"If it wasn't for Burke, who knows where we'd be right now. He got us back. He basically saved our lives because it got really hairy.

"He was an extraordinary guy."

And someone the Garcia family misses dearly.

CHERYL LADD

The serene and quiet environs of a South Dakota lake were disrupted by screams of panic when a largemouth bass attempted to drag Cheryl Ladd's older sister, Mary Ann, into the water.

Ladd barely recalls the incident since she was only three and her sister five at the time, but the story remains indelibly carved into the family tree.

"We were out in the countryside and my dad said to my sister, 'Hold my fishing pole because I have to go into the trees for a minute,'" the actress says.

"He actually had her sit on the end of it, so she didn't have to hold on to it. So she was sitting there and a huge bass suddenly was on the other end. Pretty soon, she was screaming because the fish was pulling her down into the lake. It was a pretty exciting moment. My dad came running out of the trees wondering what the heck was going on, but he grabbed her just in time. She didn't go in the water. He did lose the fishing pole, unfortunately."

ANTHONY EDWARDS

Fishing for your dinner while backpacking can be challenging and rewarding, as Anthony Edwards learned while growing up in an adventurous family of seven.

The former television star from *ER* recalls being an integral part of providing meals during the family's annual trips into the back-country of the Eastern Sierra in California and the Grand Tetons in Wyoming.

"One of the rituals was mom would bring food for the first night and for the last night, but for the three nights in-between, it was incentive to get out there with our fly rods and catch some trout," Edwards recalls.

So fishing became a big part of every trip, a true-to-life *Survivor* series.

Edwards remembers his dad teaching him and his two brothers and two sisters how to tie flies. He remembers the willow trees snagging so many of his flies. He remembers the frustration over running out of flies.

When they weren't hooking trees, they were hooking fish. For Edwards, like any kid, catching a fish was a huge thrill, but eating what he caught was *piece d' resistance*.

"My dad always made a huge deal over the fact the trout cheeks were the biggest delicacy in the world, and you could savor that," Edwards says. "So we'd get all excited about our two little trout cheeks. You'd save your cheeks for last, for dessert."

Did the family ever go without the main course? Never.

"I'm sure they had food and they weren't going to let us starve to death," Edwards says. "But you really felt like when you caught that fish and you ate it that night you were really participating in providing dinner."

NANCY O'DELL

Long before breaking into the glitter of Hollywood, Nancy O'Dell found herself in the spotlight while fishing with her father in Murrells Inlet, South Carolina.

O'Dell, 11 at the time, became the center of attention after her father found a fishing hole teeming with spots—a bottom-feeding fish that weighs a pound or two, shows up in the fall and has an attraction to Nancy's hook.

Miss Lady Luck was catching spot after spot while grizzled fishermen shook their heads in amazement nearby.

"I don't know what it was, but every time I'd throw it in, within a matter of seconds, I would catch a fish," the co-host of *Access Hollywood* recalls. "All of a sudden, all the boats kept coming in closer and closer and closer to get in on our little hole.

"It was so funny. They couldn't catch a thing and they were so angry. I remember them all asking my dad what kind of rod and reel we were using, what kind of bait we were using, how I was throwing the bait out. I was trying to take the credit—'It's me!'

"I felt so proud that I could catch all these fish with my dad and all these other men, these pro fishermen, were wanting to know what the little girl was using.

"My dad told them we had magic secrets. It was blood worms, as I recall, so I wouldn't bait the hook. I remember doing everything else. I remember reeling the fish in and taking it off the hook. I think we caught 50 or 60 fish. We were having a lot of luck that day."

To this day, the episode is O'Dell's brightest moment with a fishing rod and one of her favorite memories with her father.

BRANFORD MARSALIS

The fishing trip of a lifetime unfolded not because of what was caught but for the memories created. For world-renowned saxophonist Branford Marsalis, it was pure harmony.

Marsalis tells the story from his youth. It was the first time he traveled outside his hometown New Orleans for an extended time.

"My favorite fishing story is the first time my brother, Wynton, and I went fishing with my grandfather and my dad in the Gulf of Mexico. We'd never been on a big boat before. We were going to go for the big stuff.

"My grandfather, it was part of his continuous and, to this point, failed search for the great white trout—the big one—in the Gulf of Mexico. *He's going to get one.*

"On the way there, he fell asleep at the wheel and almost killed us. No, we were in another car, that's right. He almost killed my cousin.

"When we finally got there, we got on a boat and went out. We were fishing. The first guy to get something was Wynton. You know the story. He didn't want to be there, so he took the rod, threw it out and dropped it to the bottom, 'I got something.' He's pulling and pulling and it won't come up, won't come up. My grandfather says it's something big. It wouldn't move. My father says, 'Ah, it's a shoe, pull the line.' So we yank it and it pops loose. 'You popped my line,' Wynton says. 'Reel it in, Wynton.'

"There was something at the end of it and it was not a shoe. It was a ribbon fish, a really thin, translucent fish that is similar to eels with jaws of steel. It's a beautiful fish. They were going to throw it back because it's not edible, but they couldn't pry it off. So my grandfather says, 'All right, grab it, get the cleaver and hack the head off. 'No, that's a beautiful fish,' I was like nine or 10. It took them a lot of effort to pry it off.

"It was a great day. We never did catch the white trout, but we caught a ton of catfish, which we ate. It was the first time we'd ever caught fish, cut them there, fried them. Fresh catfish. The smell lingered in my nose and endures to this day. I'm not kidding.

"He had a sense of storytelling, my grandfather. He used to talk about these darn white trout. He would talk about them so much we couldn't wait to go get the darn things. We never got them, but it was OK. We had such a good time, sitting on the boat, hanging. It was one of those trips that I hope to one day do with my son."

GEORGE GERVIN

Hanging on the wall of George Gervin's home in San Antonio is a 14-pound rainbow trout stuffed with memories.

The fish was caught by Gervin's grandfather, William Newell, on King Salmon Lake in Alaska in 1988. It was the biggest rainbow trout ever caught on the lake, or so the story goes. Newell was 85 at the time. He passed away two years later.

"Before he died, that's all he wanted to do was go fishing," Gervin says. "He used to take me fishing when I was young. I was so proud that

I had an opportunity to take him somewhere he's never been. He was a good man and he loved fishing."

In Alaska, they fished all day for seven days. Gervin, the Basketball Hall of Fame guard, and everyone else in the area were catching salmon right and left. Except Gervin's grandfather.

"He didn't catch a fish for seven days," Gervin recalls. "He was just so glad to see me out there with him catching fish. I was catching 30- and 40-pound salmon. He didn't catch one. He kept saying, 'Fish, I know you's out there, I know you's out there.' He never got one, man, but he had a great time and never gave up.

"A month later, he went back. They loved him so much, I flew him back out there and they let him stay at the cabin for free. They fished again for seven days and he was killing them, and he brought that big, old rainbow trout to me and I said, 'Grandpa, I knew you was going to get 'im.'

"He goes back a month later and catches the biggest rainbow trout ever caught on the lake.

"That's my fish story. It ain't funny, but it's something that means a lot to me. My granddad meant everything to me. He raised me. When he went to the grave, he went to the grave with a smile, and a fish on his mind."

STEVE GATLIN

Kids say the darnedest things and sometimes the dearest things, as singer Steve Gatlin discovered in 1981 while coming home from an unsuccessful fishing trip with his then four-year-old daughter, Ashley.

On a pond at Nashville Golf and Athletic Club, his best friend and his boys were catching fish after fish, yet Gatlin couldn't get one for his daughter.

"After it was over, I was so dejected because we didn't catch anything," said Gatlin, a member of the famous country-singing trio, The Gatlin Brothers. "As we started to leave, we got in my car and were driving home, my head was down, I was thinking, 'All I want to do is catch a fish and let my little girl catch a fish.'

"She knew I was dejected. Didn't say a word. Then she looked over at me and she said, 'Dad, some day we'll catch a fish and when we do, it'll be a fine, fine day.' It melted my heart. That's all I needed right there. It was great.

"We've laughed about this ever since. 'Someday when we ever catch a fish, it'll be a fine, fine day.'"

Chapter Thirteen

Fishing Lines and Bloopers

In the production of TV fishing shows, the fish don't always do what they're supposed to do. Often they are unwilling participants. Fish don't hit a lure on cue, don't jump on cue, don't take line on cue. Putting enough fishing action on film for a half-hour episode can take hours. It can be as maddening as losing a fish at the boat.

Even when the fish are biting, things can sometimes go wrong, just as they do in the process of making a movie or TV show. Actors mess up, directors yell cut, everybody has a good laugh and they do it over again until it gets done right.

Inevitably, the cameraman keeps rolling and a comedic moment grows into a knee-slapping out-take that is probably more entertaining than the original script. How else to explain the popularity of *America's*

Funniest Home Videos, real-life moments gone hysterically wrong, and blooper shows, showing the goof-ups of paid entertainers.

Mistakes and mishaps occur while making TV fishing shows, too. Bill Dance has experienced so many in his 37 years of producing *Bill Dance Outdoors*, he's on volume three of *Bloopers and Memorable Moments* sold on video.

"People love to see people mess up," Dance says. "I'm the best in the west at that. I'm the best in the east, too. People say, 'When you going to do another blooper show?' I say, 'I could do one every week,' and I almost can."

Hank Parker, on the air 20 years with *Hank Parker's Outdoor Magazine*, is more succinct: "I *am* a blooper show."

Jimmy Houston has made his share of blunders in the 29 years of *Jimmy Houston Outdoors*, but he doesn't collect them to make blooper videos. He just puts everything that happens in each episode.

"We have things happen all the time," he says. "When you think about it, a television fishing show was the original reality television. Reality television is a big deal nowadays, and that's what fishing shows are. We start at daylight and whatever happens out on the lake, that's what we build the story with on television."

For Dance, losing three $50,000 cameras into the lake were expensive realities—all caught on tape by a second camera.

Dance knocked a cameraman out of the boat by accident when he backed up while fighting a fish. Two other times, the cameraman tripped and rolled into the lake with the camera on his shoulder.

"I kind of wondered why insurance rates went up, but I guess that's why," Dance said.

Paying closer attention might have prevented the loss of lens. It could also have saved Dance an embarrassment akin to walking out the front door having forgotten to put on pants.

After his boat was launched, Dance tried maneuvering it away with the electric trolling motor but discovered something amiss. The boat wasn't cooperating. And for good reason.

"The boat was still hooked to the trailer," Dance explains. "We didn't take the straps off. The boat was floating the trailer."

Somehow, the hitch pin came out so whomever was driving the truck pulled up the launch ramp and left the trailer behind. Dance was too busy getting his gear ready to notice the faux pax.

Since the trailer had a front wheel, Dance managed to run the boat *and trailer* far enough up the ramp to get the trailer hitched. Other than a red face, no harm was done.

Embarrassing moments are commonplace for Dance. He figures he's made 50 million casts and still he hangs lures in trees, as he did while filming one episode.

"Of course, they thought that was funny, so they kept the camera going," Dance said. "I shook the tree above me and got the bait un-hung."

The shaking brought down more than his lure, however. Like an apple shook free from a limb, a five-foot chicken snake dropped onto his head and shoulders. The rodent-eating snake was slithering all over Dance.

"I couldn't get rid of him," he says. "Every time I tried to throw him, he kept wrapping around my wrist. Finally I kicked him and he landed on the bottom of the boat. The camera caught him crawling out of the boat."

This wasn't his only wildlife adventure. Dance once hooked a black swan that eventually tried biting him, and while fishing a farm pond he found himself in the middle of a stampede of 40 longhorn cattle. Cue the *Rawhide* music.

On occasion, Dance has gotten up close to fish, too—by falling into the lake.

Dance once set the hook on a bass so hard he broke off the boat's pedestal seat and fell back into the water. Another time, he pushed off from a snag and the snag broke, sending him into frigid water of Toledo Bend.

One episode Dance did on being prepared showed him loading his boat with various pieces of equipment. When he swung the battery over to put it on the boat, the boat wasn't there—the crew inexplicably moved it. The weight of the battery carried Dance right into the drink.

"It was amazing I didn't kill myself," he says.

He has hurt himself, though. Using a large crankbait that looks like a shad on steroids, Dance set the hook on a large bass that went airborne, dislodging the lure and sending it like a torpedo straight for his face.

"I tried to block it with my hands," he recalls. "Before I could get my hands up, it shot right through my hands and hit me right in the nose."

The hook buried in the corner of his nose.

"It hurt so bad," Dance says. "The film crew thought it was hilarious."

Is it any surprise Dance is on Volume 3 of blooper tapes?

Parker, the human blooper show, was once filming a commercial about three flavors of fish formulas that anglers use to attract fish to a plastic worm. Liquorice, shad and nightcrawler were the flavors.

The formula maker wanted Parker to use the spray in an application that hadn't been done before. So Parker decided to spray a plastic worm with a fish formula, pop it into his mouth and say how much energy it gives you. He intended to use the liquorice flavor.

"Well, it was hotter than the Fourth of July and I sprayed that dadgum nightcrawler formula and popped it in my mouth, and it was all I could do to keep from throwing up," he recalls.

The cameraman was laughing so hard, the camera was jiggling, but it captured the blooper that continued with Parker spitting out the formula and gargling with Coca-Cola in an attempt to erase the taste in his mouth.

The fish formula maker never did get the commercial he was hoping for. But he got one heckuva blooper.

"I've probably had more people comment about that little blooper over the years than I ever imagined," Parker says. "It was a big mistake to put that nightcrawler formula into your mouth. I was going to use the liquorice formula. It's not too bad, but the nightcrawler formula, I think they put real nightcrawlers in it."

Like Parker, Al Lindner of *Lindner's Angling Edge* made a blooper while filming a commercial, only his was broadcast on the air. In fact, the 30-second spot wound up winning awards.

"The whole thing was a complete accident," Lindner says.

Nearly 20 years ago, Trilene fishing line ran a campaign and the tagline was, "I can't believe a line this thin can be this strong."

In the print version that ran in magazines, a photo showed an angler leaning over a branch and holding the line, pulling a bass out of the water and weeds. Lindner was enlisted to be the angler in the TV version.

A big-time production company from New York went to Lindner's hometown in Minnesota, found an ideal spot and the perfect branch, set up the lighting and was ready to shoot.

Lindner leaned over the branch and grabbed the line with the bass. As he was readying to deliver his line, the branch broke and down into the cold water he fell. He came up holding the bass and looking into the camera and the producer's eyes.

"What flashed through my mind was, 'Hey, say something dummy,'" Lindner recalls.

So he chuckled and said, "I can't believe a line this thin can be this strong," and then busted up.

"Did you get that?" the producer asked the cameraman.

"Yeah," the cameraman replied.

"Good, let's pack up and go home," the producer said.

The whole thing took 20 seconds, but the spot was used for years. It was the only time Lindner had fallen into the water in front of a camera. Knock on wood, he still hasn't lost a camera or cameraman overboard in 32 years of producing TV fishing shows.

"We've been pretty lucky in that area," Lindner says.

Jerry McKinnis has never fallen into the water or lost a camera in 37 years of filming *The Fishin' Hole*, the longest-running outdoors show, but he almost lost a cameraman.

Coach Bobby Knight and McKinnis were fishing from a canoe in the Minnesota-Canadian boundary waters in the early 1990s. They were trying to catch smallmouth bass. Knight was fly fishing with a popping bug, a technique not mastered by many.

The anglers and crew found a little bay with a pocket that looked like it held a fish. They spent 20 minutes positioning the boats and camera angles to ensure the best lighting. Then Knight started casting.

Sure enough, a fish was there waiting. The four-pounder exploded on the popper, made one jump and spit it out. As the ripples in the water settled, a tidal wave was building.

Breaking the quiet, cameraman Mark deLinde quipped, "Eddie Sutton would've caught that fish."

Knight glared back at deLinde and picked up a paddle.

"Coach just picked up the paddle and threw it across the little bay at this cameraman," McKinnis recalls with a laugh. "That paddle just went whizzing through the air."

"You little son of a bitch, you haven't been working for McKinnis long enough to talk to me like that," Knight shot back.

Like Coach Sutton, Knight had been a guest on *The Fishin' Hole* several times, so he and deLinde were known for going round and round in mostly friendly face-offs.

"He didn't cower at all," McKinnis said of deLinde. "He was ready to do battle."

This would have made for a pretty good blooper, only the camera wasn't rolling. The cameraman was too busy ducking.

Another behind-the-scenes incident involving McKinnis that never made it to tape was the time in a tiny town near Akron, Ohio, when he was arrested for no reason other than he didn't have proper ID.

McKinnis beat his crew to town and jogged to a corner to greet the truck. Police officers arrived and asked him what he was doing.

"I'm not doing anything," he replied.

They kept asking questions and were acting rudely, McKinnis says. Finally, they told him he needed to show some identification.

"Why, I don't either," McKinnis told them.

Since he was in a jogging suit, he didn't have his billfold. To the policemen, that was the last straw. They pushed McKinnis against the wall, handcuffed him and hauled him off to jail.

McKinnis was so upset he refused to answer any questions at the jailhouse. Finally he told them to bring that day's newspaper and then he'd answer their questions. They obliged.

The TV host then pointed at the photo on the front page. It was McKinnis and an accompanying story about him coming to town to shoot an episode of his show.

"Right there is the guy you just arrested down there on the corner for not having any identification," he told the police.

Embarrassed, the police let him go, but not before the sheriff arrived with his grandchildren to obtain autographs from McKinnis.

"I thought, 'This is a fine kettle of beans, I'm in jail and here you're coming for autographs,'" McKinnis says. "We were all laughing at that time. We weren't laughing at it about the time I got handcuffed, I guarantee."

Seems the police were on the lookout for an area burglar and tabbed McKinnis as the suspect.

A thief of a different kind was the subject of a blooper from *Inside Sportfishing*, hosted by Michael Fowlkes, who has longed to produce a show catching and releasing a swordfish.

The opportunity presented itself in the waters off East Cape in Baja California, when while trolling for marlin, the telltale sign of a swordfish materialized. A dorsal fin broke the surface like a periscope from a submarine. Behind it, half the tail waved back and forth.

"Swordfish!" Fowlkes yelled.

Elmer Alfafara, developer of a state-of-the-art drag system for Shimano, made a perfect cast, tossing a bait toward the swordfish, considered the Holy Grail of sportfishing.

"He's turning," Fowlkes yelled, focusing the camera on the prized gamefish. "He's on it!"

But before the swordfish could gobble up the bait, a striped marlin shot up from below and stole it from under the swordie's nose.

"I thought the swordfish was going to chase the marlin down and kill him," Fowlkes said. That was probably what Fowlkes wanted to do, because it was the closest he's come to filming a swordfish hookup.

When filming a fishing show, directing a fish is like trying to catch a salmon in a trout net. It's near impossible. But it can make for some interesting bloopers.

We leave you with some famous last words and fishing lines from several celebrities as they give their personal take on fishing. Some might even be considered bloopers.

TIGER WOODS
Plays golf for a living, fishes for a hobby

"Fly fishing is like golf in that you have to find a rhythm to increase your chance of success. On my first trip to Ireland with my good friend Mark O'Meara, I had a hard time finding my rhythm, but I managed to land a few browns and rainbows. I've been hooked ever since. I love it for many reasons. One is that you can get away and just hang out with friends. My fishing tips? Forget about everything and just enjoy it, be ready to hook a fish on every cast and look out for unexpected visitors like bears, which like fish, too...but that's another story."

BOBBY KNIGHT

Renowned college basketball coach,
a.k.a. the General

"The last thing I did with my dad before he passed away was go fishing. I taught my two boys how to fish and we go fishing all the time. Fishing in a family situation enables a dad—I think—to really have something special with his kids, that if he teaches his kids how to fish, you got somebody to fish with until you die.

"Why fishing? I just like it. It's competitive. It gives you a chance to match your wits with the quarry, i.e. the fish. You've got to learn how to read the water and deliver the fly, and have reflexes to catch the fish.

"I think catching a fish on a fly is like making a basket or getting a hit or sinking a putt. It always gives me that kind of pleasure, and it's something that I've been able to do.

"The thing that I've always appreciated—and I'm not sure why— but I never ever get upset when I lose a fish. I might say 'damn,' but that never bothers me because I always feel like the fish won. And there's always another fish there."

GEORGE LOPEZ

Award-winning comedian and
star of TV show **George Lopez**

"People go crazy about fishing. We were doing a movie one time in New Mexico and these guys were fly fishing and they went crazy for it. I thought, 'Wow, what is it about this sport that these guys just love it?' These guys were driving like six hours to go fishing and coming back and then working. Whatever that is, it's probably what golf is to me."

TROY AIKMAN

Former star quarterback of
Super Bowl-winning Dallas Cowboys

"Fishing is something to do when the weather's not good enough to go golfing or you can't get a tee time. Then you go fishing.

Bobby Knight, as a youngster, sitting on a dock with
his father, Pat, whom he enjoyed fishing with.
Photo courtesy of Bobby Knight

"I went on a big trip to Lake Fork [Texas] one time and it was supposed to be the bass capital of the world. We fished all day. Finally, we caught one little bitty one, me and another buddy. We each caught a little fish.

"If they're biting, I guess like anybody, I really enjoy it. But I just don't find anything appealing to just be sitting out there on the water. I can't stand it. And no one can guarantee me that the fish are biting before I go. So I don't even usually waste my time."

TOMMY SMOTHERS
One-half of the Smothers Brothers comedy team

"We used to fish with my grandfather down in Lake Rodriguez just south of Tijuana. We'd bring back 200 or 300 fish. You know, bluegill, crappie and bass. Of course Dickie and I were eight or nine and we were the cleaners. About three years in a row, each year we got stuck cleaning the fish. Catfish, they keep moving all the time, even when you're cleaning them.

"The first four or five you're, 'Oh man, how are we going to get through this?'

"My grandpa would go out with his older son, and Dickie and I would stay with grandma on the shore with a pole. They'd go out trolling real slow for the big ones. We caught the biggest sitting on shore. It really got grandpa mad because we're sitting there with a bamboo pole and using our minnows. We got four bass and one was a five-pounder. It really upset him because he's out there with all the trick stuff."

DAN QUAYLE
Former United States Vice-President

"If I get the opportunity, I really enjoy fly fishing because there's so much skill to it. You've got to get prepared. You've got to read the water. You've got to put the right fly on. It's a real art. I like hanging around good fly fishermen. I learn every time I go out. It's something like golf because there's so much to fly fishing. Casting is one thing, but fly fishing is a whole different level. I don't get a lot of time to do it, but I sure enjoy it."

FUZZY ZOELLER
Professional golfer and funny man

"I got a six-acre pond behind my house. I've always heard of people catching two fish on one lure. As much as I've fished, I have never done it. My son did it twice in one night.

"It was just crazy. I said, 'You know Miles, that's like making a hole in one.' He looked at me and he thought it was easy. About 15 minutes later, damned if he didn't do it again. That's the first time in my life that I've seen that done and I've been fishing since I was about eight years old.

"He couldn't wait to jump out of the boat and go to the house and tell his mother what he had done."

TONY DANZA

Known for comedic roles in sitcoms
Taxi and Who's the Boss

"My father was a garbage man for the city of New York. He had a bunch of friends and we'd get up early and drive out to Captree on Long Island. We'd go out on a party-boat for fluke and flounder. Every once in a while if I was real good, he'd take me for bluefish. I guess my most memorable moment was just eating a salami sandwich on that boat going up and down. It was pretty rough."

BILL MURRAY

Comedian of Caddyshack and
Ghostbusters fame

"I'm not much of a fisherman. I eat fish, but I don't catch it."

WILLIAM DEVANE

Actor best known for role on Knot's Landing

"I do mostly fly fishing in streams. I'm not that nuts [about it]. But I've floated the Yellowstone a number of times and I've fished up through Utah, quietly by myself. I like to fly fish, but I'm not avid. If I had a choice between fishing and playing golf, I'd play golf."

ARNOLD PALMER

Golfing great known as The King

"I have a few stories but none that I would want you to put into print."

TOBY KEITH

Award-winning country music star

"I've got a catfish story where we put out like 16 cane poles along the Arkansas River and put live perch on them, and catch those big flatheads—50, 60, 70 pounds. It's called pole lining. We were on a trip up there one time and ran out of perch.

"Somewhere along the way, a shad swam up alongside our boat. He was a wounded shad. I netted him up. He was barely breathing. I stuck him on the very last hook just for fun and we caught about a 42-pound catfish on that last hook."

IVAN LENDL

Former tennis great

"A friend of mine asked me what it'll take for him to get me to go fishing. I told him, 'When I win the British Open, I'll fish with you half a day.'

"That means I'm not going fishing."

MIKE MODANO

National Hockey League star

"I'm a big fan of deep-sea fishing. I like the ocean. I like just grabbing a boat and floating out there and trolling around. I enjoy it a lot."

EDWIN MOSES
Two-time Olympic gold-medal winning hurdler

"I grew up fishing in Ohio. There was a lake about a half mile from my house. My father taught us how to fish very early. I had baitcasting reels and used to fish all the time during the summer. In fact, we had a fishing club—me, my two brothers and two other guys in the neighborhood. We used to fish all the time, bring them home, fry them, do the works."

DAVID ROBINSON
Former NBA star and Navy graduate

"My father was in the navy while I was growing up. He used to take me to the piers and we'd drop bait through the holes in the pier and fish off the side. It would be great fishing. You catch them nonstop. That's where I kind of learned to enjoy fishing."

JOHNNY BENCH
Hall-of-Fame catcher of Cincinnati Reds

"I grew up fishing with my dad on the Washita River down in Oklahoma. We used to catch a lot of catfish. Mom was the best cook in the world. We had so much fried catfish. It was so good. And he'd take us bass fishing and trot-lining for flatheads, but catfish was the No. 1 source fish in Oklahoma.

"The first time I went trout fishing was with Bobby Knight in Montana and the second time we went was at the Green River at the Flaming Gorge Lodge.

"Flaming Gorge Lodge at Green River. Trout fishing. Bobby Knight. It can't get better than that. Nothing. Nothing. He's world class and fish are everywhere and it's challenging and it's wonderful and I caught some nice cutthroat, big cutthroat, about five or six pounds.

"It was just perfect. They say for every hour you fish you gain a day in life."

BRYANT GUMBEL

Award-winning television personality

"Not at all, not at all, I don't fish in the least."

JOHN BRODIE

Former NFL star quarterback turned senior pro golfer

"I went out to fish one time and got scared I might catch one and quit."

CRAIG T. NELSON

Actor known for TV series Coach

"The only story I can remember is going out bass fishing with my dad just before he died. We stayed out there, it must have been six hours. We stayed out there so long that my dad almost got second-degree burns. I remember both he and my mom were just really burnt. We didn't catch a thing and I didn't get a bite.

"It was nice just being able to go out with him and do what he loved to do. He was a big fisherman. I didn't fish much after that."

FLEX ANDERSON

Star of TV sitcom One on One

"I'm hydrophobic so you won't catch me in a boat. Hydrophobia is the fear of water. I can't do boats and stuff like that. I almost drowned twice as a kid, so that put the fear of God in me. Once I almost drowned twice, I was like, 'You know what? Except for the shower, me and water, we don't do too well. That's it.'"

DARIUS RUCKER
Lead singer of Hootie & the Blowfish

"I've fished before. The guys in my band all have boats and go out.
"My very first time fishing was in my 20s. Me and Deano [Felber], who plays bass in the band, we were in Key West and we drove out and went to this little fishing place and we got rods and everything. We went to a place where you look in the water and you could see thousands of fish. I never had any experience with fishing. We're going and I see this really big fish. I'm not really sure what it is. I cast out to it and the fish hits, and as soon as I set the hook, the fish jumps up and bites the line and is gone. Dean freaked out. It was a barracuda. It was like, whoa, I didn't know what the hell I was catching I was just going after fish. That was pretty wild."

DENNIS HAYSBERT
Golden Globe nominee from TV drama 24

"I have fished, but I am not a fisherman."

BRETT HULL
Former National Hockey League star

"I don't fish. Life's too short."

MARIO LOPEZ
Rising star known for role on sitcom **Saved by the Bell**

"I went out on a half-day boat off Los Angeles and caught a big bar-racuda. I was reeling it in and all of a sudden this sea lion jumped out of the water and grabbed the fish and started tugging away at it. I'm tug-owarring with this sea lion and the sea lion eventually won. It was so funny because it would mess with me. He'd let me have it and then he'd grab it and then he'd let me have it. Then he tore my line off. I went home and said, 'I had a fish this big,' and the reaction was 'Yeah, yeah.' But I really did have a fish."

DIGGER PHELPS

College basketball analyst and former Notre Dame basketball coach

"The great thing about fishing is you really learn to get mellow and it humbles you and it makes you slow down. That's the great thing about it.

"You feel the stress and tension leave your body.

"I'm an avid fisherman. I love to do it when I can. It's a great sport."

ROBIN YOUNT

Baseball Hall-of-Famer from Milwaukee Brewers

"Bob Uecker and I went bass fishing a few times at spring training outside Phoenix. He was trying to catch fish just about everywhere but in the water. He fished more on land than in the water. He kept trying to convince me that that's where the fish were.

"He didn't catch a lot of fish that day. There were other things about that story, but I just remember most of his casts didn't hit water."

DAN RATHER

Retired CBS anchorman

"I would be delighted to oblige you by sharing my best fish story with you, but I have to tell you, I don't think you'd enjoy the results. As a reporter, I must never exaggerate, or fudge, or color, or stretch the truth, or embroider the details, or do any of the things that make fish stories so...lively.

"You might not have thought there was a conflict of interest between journalism and fishing, but there you have it. No matter the whoppers my fishing buddies are spinning, I am simply forbidden to join in. It's more frustrating than eating soup with a fork, it really is. My hands are tied—literally. I can't even put my thumb on the scale when I'm weighing the fish.

"I can, however, tell you honestly that all of my best fish are the ones that got away—because I catch and release."

MICHAEL CHANG

Former tennis great

"I was fishing earlier than I was playing tennis. It was something we always enjoyed as a family. Mom would pack a picnic lunch and we'd spend a day out fishing.

"I used to have a small Snoopy rod when I was young. You'd take three big rocks and prop it up. I propped mine up. My mom had baited

Former tennis great Michael Chang poses with a chum salmon caught on the Skokomish River in Washington during a fall run.
Photo courtesy of the Chang Family Foundation

it with some dough mixed up with corn, fishing for carp. Carp get pretty big. I walked over to get a sandwich from my mom. All of a sudden, I hear my rod go down. I'm looking over there. My rod comes off the bank and it goes swish, plunk. I go, 'Oops, I lost my rod.' The fish took it right in.

"I just like plain fishing. It doesn't necessarily have to do with any kind of species.

"It's a nice thing not only to spend time with the family, but to be out there enjoying the atmosphere, the environment and nature, and all of God's creatures. If you catch a fish, it's a bonus.

"It's nice to just sit and be in one location for a while and not have to think so much. Fishing is one of those places I can do that. You can be out on the lake and you're away from the hustle and bustle of life. You look around, things are very peaceful, very tranquil, very opposite of tennis.

"To this day, it's always something we really enjoy."